The Privileged Woman

Cover art work by Nick LeGuern

The Privileged Woman by Joy Haney
© 1982 Radiant Life Publications
Sixth Printing, June 1996, Revised Edition

Printed in the United States of America

ISBN #1-880969-14-9

Table of Contents

Foreword
Introduction
Preface

Dedication

This book is lovingly dedicated to my mother-in-law, Olive F. Haney, who is both a minister's wife and a great example, and with loving memories to my mother who has gone on to be with the Lord. She was a woman of God and had a consecration that was unexcelled.

These are two great virtuous women.

Foreword

Emerging from the vast fellowship of the United Pentecostal Church, which is extended to the four corners of the earth, is a group of young pastors and their helpmeets. *Helpmeet* is a very interesting word. It is not to be misconstrued as *helpmate*. Rather, it describes the very beautiful plan that God intended that man should enjoy. It refers to the supplemental role that a woman would play in the life of a man. This is perhaps greatly extended in the very specific role that a pastor's or minister's wife fulfills.

As the title of this book suggests, to be a minister's wife is not a burden but a privilege. Joy Haney is a symbol of the emerging young women who, if the Lord tarries, will be great forces of influence for the future ministerial work that will be done through capable people.

This book will introduce you to the areas of life in which this privileged woman works: in a church, with her children, in creative areas and in all the valued, interesting levels of dimensional beauty where those who have been called to do this specific task will function. If there ever was a position of importance, the minister's wife displays a solid example of inspirational leadership. If she should ever fail to realize the vast significance of her calling, she could devastate a God-called man.

You will enjoy these writings because they are coming from a very outstanding young minister's wife who knows what it is to rear children, to stand by her husband in his numerous duties, to smile when the clouds hang low, to be friendly to the friendless, and to lift up the spirit of the distressed, though her own problems may be greater than those she assists in her call as a minister's wife.

To those who are fulfilling this great dimension of ministry, we would urge you to read this carefully. Read it prayerfully and then take the excellent direction that has been given from the experience of Joy Haney, and apply it to your own life and go forth with hope and not with fear. There is a need today in our pressure-packed society to have reading of this nature.

Joy, as she is known affectionately by her friends, has given you not only a well-written treatise, but she has also given you what her name implies. It is not only a privilege but it is a "joy" to be the wife of a minister.

Rev. & Mrs. Nathaniel A. Urshan
1982

Introduction

You are privileged because you get to live with a man who is called of God. You get to share in helping make the world a better place in which to live, and in helping bring men, women, and children the gospel of salvation. You get to witness despair turned into hope and see homes put back together because of the miracle power of Jesus Christ. You are treated special because you are a minister's wife. You get to partake of all the goodies and gifts that come your way over and over again at Christmas time and other holidays. Your birthday is celebrated. People look up to you. Your anniversary is not forgotten, and the flowers are many. You are loved by a lot of people because of your position, but after they get to know you, you should be loved because of you. That is why you want to be the best you can be for God, so you can influence others toward both Him and a better way of life.

There are also painful experiences in being a minister's wife. There will be jealous whisperers and gossipers who will attack the leadership of you and your husband, and there will be the spiritual attack of the devil upon the ministry because of the effectiveness of the gospel. There will be failures, heartaches, and other hard experiences, but when you know you are chosen to be the wife of a God-called man in a special ministry, the advantages outweigh the disadvantages and call for the best in you to be brought forth by the power of Jesus Christ. You can never say it is easy to be a minister's wife, no matter how rewarding such a life may be. I hope this book can help you to adjust to a "different" way of life and help you to see your responsibility to God and to your position.

Preface

The following words, spoken by missionary David Livingstone, will indict many Christians who are filled with the Holy Spirit. I wish to put emphasis upon his attitude and surrender to God. He said:

People talk of the sacrifice I have made in spending so much of my life in Africa. Can that be called a sacrifice which is simply paid back as a small part of the great debt owing to our God, which we can never repay? Is that a sacrifice which brings its own reward of healthful activity, the consciousness of destiny hereafter?

Away with such a word, such a view, and such a thought! It is emphatically no sacrifice. Say rather it is a privilege. Anxiety, sickness, suffering or danger now and then, with a foregoing of the common conveniences and charities of this life, may make us pause and cause the spirit to waver and sink; but let this only be for a moment. All these are nothing when compared with the glory which shall hereafter be revealed in and for us. I never made a sacrifice. Of this we ought not to talk when we remember the great sacrifice which He made to give Himself for us.

1

You and Your God

"Thou shalt love the Lord thy God with ALL thine heart and with all thy soul, and with all thy might" (Deuteronomy 6:5)

Your relationship with God is the most important aspect of your life, for this colors all other relationships. If you look upon Him long enough, He becomes a mirror to your soul and you start taking on His characteristics and showing forth His attitudes. In your prostrate position at His feet, you will feel His love flow from His heart into your heart. His power will surge through your spiritual blood veins, giving you strength to do what He commands you to do.

Your closet time is number one. How can you know someone if you do not spend time with him? You may hear good things about a person, see him from afar, but never communicate with that individual, therefore, there is not a cemented bond of friendship. There have been times when I longed to deepen a friendship with a certain individual, but the opportunity never came to be with that person very often, so I was left with that longing unfulfilled. We have all desired to become

13

better acquainted with Christ and plan to do so someday, but somehow when we come away inspired from conferences and camps, we still roll the desire ahead. Oftentimes all we want is a superficial relationship with God when He is wanting to hold us close to His bosom like he did John, the Beloved. It is important to set aside a certain time each day to spend with the Lover of your soul, Jesus. "But it is good for me to draw near to God...." (Psalm 73:28).

The Lord should be in your subconscious thoughts constantly. It is good to form the habit of always mentally either praying about some need or giving thanks to Him. Prayer should be your very breath. If it takes setting the alarm and getting up early to pray, do it. Please, do not neglect the most important part of your day. The time of washing your soul clean, sweeping away the cobwebs of doubt, and tearing out the small erosions of impurity should be utmost in your daily schedule. Take time to love and be loved by God and to be inspired and filled with His power.

Prayer to God not only gives you power to overcome evil and sin, but it gives you creative power and inspirational thoughts. Prayer is the greatest force of power in the world—it is the most powerful form of energy one can generate. The lack of prayer is as a sleeping giant in many homes, and the result is frustration, confusion, a lack of victory, and general irritations. If people could learn the enormous force of power and victory that comes from praying each day, they could replace a lot of nasty tempers, gossipy tongues, heartaches, and broken dreams, with new goals, visions, dreams, and accomplishments. God wants to answer the prayers of His saints. He is waiting with thousands of angels to do just that. "For the eyes of the Lord run to and fro throughout the whole earth, to shew himself strong in the behalf of them whose heart is perfect toward him" (II Chronicles 16:9).

There is also a need for deeper prayer in these last days, including travailing and intercessory prayer. The scripture says, "If my people, which are called by my name, shall humble themselves, and pray, and seek my face, and turn from their wicked ways; then will I hear from heaven, and will forgive their sin, and will heal their land" (II Chronicles 7:14). Prayer is the *greatest* thing you can do for your minister husband and the Kingdom of God. Women who will wail and weep over the lost and wayward ones and the furthering of God's kingdom will always be needed. This kind of prayer takes strength from you and makes you lay weakly at His feet, exhausted from the anguish of your soul, but this kind of prayer always gets answered!

Prayer clears the vision, steadies the nerves, defines duty, stiffens the purpose, and sweetens and strengthens the spirit. Jesus, being our great example, gave us a plain view of His habits. It was a custom with Him to rise early and pray each morning. He seemed to choose a quiet time when the noises of earth were hushed. He not only had a regular time to pray, but He also prayed before and after special events in His ministry. Mark 1:35 gives a good example: "And in the morning, rising up a great while before day, he went out, and departed into a solitary place, and there prayed."

Situations will occur that make it impossible for you to keep your prayer time at the exact moment you have set aside for it.

There will be times when you will be up most of the night with a sick child or saint, or when you get in very late from a preaching engagement. You need to use good sense and get your rest, or you will not be able to perform all your duties that day. The Lord understands, and you can pray in your heart while you are doing your work.

Deuteronomy 5:7, "Thou shalt have none other gods before me," is one of the first and foremost commandments. God wants to be Lord of each life, heart, and substance. "Seek ye first the kingdom of God, and his righteousness; and all these things shall be added unto you" (Matthew 6:33). Do first things first and the secondary things will fall into their rightful place, and all of your needs will be met. "Thou shalt **worship** the Lord thy God, and him only shalt thou serve" (Matthew 4:10). He says to not serve the god of money, materialism, selfish gain, or prestige, but make Him number one; then He promised to give everything else that is needed.

Sacrifice even though you do not feel like it and God will repay you one-hundred fold. Give of yourself through fasting and dying to self, and God will bless your efforts over and over again. Say, "Lord, I give you everything. Take all that I have and make something that will bring glory to You. Use me to help others find You and reach their potential in God."

Often in the midst of giving yourself totally to God there will be times when pressure pushes down upon you, because Satan will try to stop you from doing so. Black clouds will try to close in, and life might seem one big heartache. It is then time to "Be still and know that I am God" (Psalm 46:10). The Lord is your strength and He will be with you. During this time He sometimes sends a ray of sunshine from unexpected sources: the angelic smile of a golden-haired child, the warm embrace of a caring friend, the listening ear of a dear friend, the solitude of His handiwork, the trees and streams—yes, He gives comfort and love through many avenues. Be open to His ministrations unto you through not only these, but also through His great comforting spirit which overshadows you and dwells inside of you, being ever near during the trials in your life. No matter what happens, keep drawing near to Jesus with a made-up mind and you will win over Satan and the pressure to make you stop.

As sure as the hummingbirds flutter their wings flitting from flower to flower, as sure as the English walnuts are harvested every October, God's promises to you are just as sure year after year. He will be as real and as close to you as you will allow Him to be. His gentle presence is there, nudging, prodding, loving and meeting your emotional needs as well as your spiritual needs. As you draw closer to Him, He will reward you, for "The Lord is good unto them that wait for him, to the soul that seeketh him" (Lamentations 3:25).

The **second** most important thing in your relationship with God is the reading of the Bible. You have no choice about it if you want to grow into the person God had in mind when He created you. It is a must! After wiping the spidery webs of discontent, sin and doubt from your mind and cleansing your soul through prayer, you must fill it with something. You are what you read and feed upon. The Bible should be the number one book in your life. It has jewels of wisdom in it and shines light upon questioning doubts that lurk in your mind. It purifies and comforts. It should be read with love and reverence and you

17

should devour it like you would a French eclair—with eagerness and enjoyment. You should look upon the Bible with excitement and hold it close to you, letting its wisdom control your thoughts and actions.

After you have spent time each day in the Word, then you should allow time for good inspirational reading that uplifts and prods to greater heights. You do yourself, God and your husband an injustice when you do not keep your mind inspired by the reading of the Word and other good books. These should color your conversation, for they are positive and will uplift and give hope.

How can you reach your potential in God if you do not read His instructions? How can you think on things that are lovely, true, honest, just, of good report and pure if you do not fix your mind upon the greatest source of purity and righteousness found in the Word?

I think it is very immature for a minister's wife to fill her mind constantly with romance novels and nothing else. You will go no higher in your thinking and potential until you graduate from froth-and-foam reading to the Word that will last forever. Do you desire to be a better person and to be used more of God? Then ask yourself, "What am I feeding upon?" Couple together positive prayer and positive reading, and the sky is the limit to where your thoughts and actions can soar. *Be an eagle!* Fly above the norm and become the person God created you to be. Have a close relationship with Him. Get your instructions and strength for the day from Him and you will not be as prone to waste time and energies that could be more productive. He will cause you to get your priorities right. Everything will change because your mind will be motivated to higher heights. The question is, are you going to continue in your rut and be half of a person, or are you going to reach your potential in God? You alone hold the key.

2

You and Your Husband

"She will do him good all the days of her life"
(Proverbs 31:12)

Your husband should be your best friend! With each anniversary you are building a relationship that draws you closer together. If this is not happening in your marriage it is possible to work through difficulties, but both partners must join together in their efforts for this to happen. The difference between a good marriage and a poor one is based on the following six things.

1. TRUST

Trust with an inviolable trust. You cannot build a marriage on suspicion or jealousy. You must love and **trust**. You may shake your head and say, "You do not know my husband." I will agree there are a few husbands who make it difficult for their wives to trust them. This is where you do your part, then go the second mile and leave it all in the hands of a just God. It is important to pray, love, trust, and let him have his freedom. Your husband needs to have his public time, his fellowship with the men, and his time of relaxing. He will probably choose to do some of his relaxing with you. Do not tie him down by a feeling of overpossessiveness or mistrust. Let him know you are behind him and **believe in him**, and that he is the greatest man in the world. Then treat him as such. Do not compare him with other men. Every man is important in his own right, but to you, your husband is the most important man in the world.

2. EDIFICATION

Edify and build him up. I Corinthians 8:1 says, "Charity edifieth." Tell him he is great. Encourage him, for there is a need in your husband's life to be reverenced and loved. Ephesians 5:33 in the New Living Bible reads, "Let the wife see that she respects and reverences her husband; that she notices him, regards him, honors him, prefers him, venerates and esteems him; that she defers to him, praises him, and loves and admires him exceedingly."

He needs to hear you express how proud you are of him, how much you love him, and how thankful you are for all the things he has provided for you. Instead of always whining for more, being unthankful and generally selfish, seek to change into a happy, contented, thankful wife. If you would like further study about the wife and her responsibilities, submission and reverence, there is more of a complete study in my book, *The Radiant Woman*. Take a look at yourself through the eyes of your husband. What does he see? Does he see a godly, contented, well-groomed, cheerful, pleasant wife, or does he see a frowning, grumbling, lazy wife with a tongue prone to gossip? Are you a hindrance or an asset? If a wife is commanded in Ephesians to:

respect	prefer
reverence	esteem
notice	praise
regard	love
honor	admire exceedingly

her husband, how can there be any place for continual grumbling and tearing down? This is God's formula for a successful relationship. He made man; therefore, He knows his innermost needs and made woman to fulfill those needs. A woman has needs also, and God made man to fulfill those needs. If a wife will do her part of the bargain, it will make it much easier for the husband to do what God commanded him to do. It would be hard for a husband to love a sloppy, hateful, sharp-tongued, jealous wife, so seek to make yourself and your spirit lovable. Although man and woman were made to fulfill each other's needs to a point, there is no one person that can fill all of your needs. The only one that can is the Lord Jesus. There is no disappointment in Jesus; He is your true fulfillment!

3. FORGIVENESS

Forgive with humility. "And be ye kind one to another, tenderhearted, forgiving one another, even as God for Christ's sake hath forgiven you" (Ephesians 4:32). It is easy for the human nature to hold a grudge. It almost feels good to cherish grudges in order to make the other person suffer. Because the spirit has been wounded, it wants to wound back by being cold and unforgiving. Sometimes it is difficult for adults to forgive.

Paul said, "...In malice, be ye children" (I Corinthians 14:20). Children can argue one minute and be buddies the next. The very thing that caused Lucifer to fall from heaven is the very thing that causes forgiveness to be slow in coming: *pride*. It is the fleshly nature that wars against the spirit. It is so important to get rid of grudges and resentments in order to keep a happy flow of communication between you and your husband. Your relationship with him will affect the congregation, for you give forth vibes either of love and caring or of strife and woe.

I heard the story about the young girl who, after being married for awhile, ran home to her grandma who had raised her. Grandma's advice to her was, "You married him for better or for worse, child. You've had the better; now go back to him and love him through the worse and the better will come again. And don't forget to pray, child. You will find it easier to love him better if you pray for him more." This is pretty good advice.

The fragrance of love *can* fill your house. Love is a spendthrift. It gives and demands no return. True love is not sentimental affection which may change with the circumstances, but it is a deliberate, conscious seeking of the welfare and best interest of the loved one. You should *grow* in love and understanding. As you mature in the Lord so will you mature in your love for each other. It will bind you together when you are apart. You will learn to gloss over his faults and to focus on his qualities.

It is not the will of God for you to have strife and bitterness in your home, for the minister must first be partaker of the Word of God and allow Christ to rule there. You *can* live together in peace and harmony and live a happy fulfilled life. If there are misunderstandings between you and your husband, and resentment is welling up within your heart, the following poem should be read and its message should be a constant reminder of the folly of pride.

FORGIVENESS

My heart was heavy for its
    trust had been
Abused, its kindness answered
    with foul wrong;
So, turning gloomily from my
    fellow-men,
One summer Sabbath day I
    strolled among
The green mounds of the village
    burial-place
Where, pondering how all human
    love and hate
Find one sad level; and how,
    soon or late,
Wronged and wrongdoer, each
    with meekened face,

25

And cold hands folded
    over a still heart,
Pass the green threshold of our
    common grave,
Whither all footsteps tend,
    whence none depart,
Awed for myself,
    and pitying my race,
Our common sorrow, like a
    mighty wave,
Swept all my **PRIDE** away, and
    trembling I forgave![1]

4. TAKING TIME

Take time for each other. This is very important in your re-
lationship. You must take time for just the two of you to be to-
gether every once in awhile. You grow together by being with
each other, talking and bringing each other up on all the inter-
esting things that are happening in your lives. Take time away
from the pressures of the church, the telephone, your children,
and anything else that is important to you; yes, take time to be
alone together.

We once had a wonderful couple in our home. After two
weeks of being together with them, with all the extra responsi-
bilities crowding in upon us, I felt the need to just sit down and
talk with my husband alone. So I called him at the church one
day and said, "Honey, tonight let's go to our favorite
restaurant. I need to talk to you." We left the children with our

oldest daughter and told the couple that we had to take care of some things and left. We almost felt like a couple of teenagers sneaking away from everyone. We went down to the dimly-lit restaurant right on the water and sat in our private corner and just talked and talked. We sat there for three hours just relaxing in each other's presence and catching up on everything. We had a blast. We were cementing our relationship and becoming better friends. We were not just being responsible to each other, but enjoying one another's company. He loved it and, needless to say, so did I.

Love is a magic that drives you on through toil and hardship with the anticipation of spending time in the presence of the one you love. It oils the machinery and makes things run smoother. Love looks beyond the faults, sees the potential and helps to nourish one to greater heights. It puts wings on your hands and feet, making it possible to race through a dreary job because you are doing it for the one you love. It takes boredom out of the ordinary and transforms it into a happy game of excitement.

THE MAGIC OF LOVE

Love is like magic
    And it always will be,
For love still remains
    Life's sweet mystery!

Love works in ways
    That are wondrous and strange
And there's nothing in life

That love cannot change.

Love can transform
The most commonplace
Into beauty and splendor
And sweetness and grace!

Love is unselfish
Understanding and kind,
For it sees with its heart
And not with its mind!

Love is the answer
That everyone seeks—
Love is the language
That everyone speaks.

Love can't be bought
It is priceless and free
Love like pure magic
Is a sweet mystery![2]

Another important way of keeping romance in your mar-
riage and boredom out of it is **mini-vacations**. My husband is
the one that usually plans these. Every once in awhile he will
come in and say, "Honey, can you get away for a couple of
days?" I always try to go along with his suggestion and do
everything necessary to get the children taken care of and other
things organized so we can get away. We have two or three

places where we love to go. We get into the car and the farther we go the more we feel the pressures melt away. On one occasion, we stayed near the mountains in a quaint and beautiful motel. In the evening we walked down the little street and bought big old-fashioned ice cream cones. We took our time strolling down the street and then walked back, hand-in-hand totally relaxed, without getting in a hurry. What a great time we had those two days enjoying life's simple pleasures!

Not only should you take periodic breaks and celebrate your love, but you should celebrate your anniversary in a special way each year. Put meaning into it. Always remember each other's birthday and other special occasions and make them memorable. Then the everydays of life can also mean much to each of you if you will seek to please each other and put a smile in the other's heart.

5. SERVICE

Love by serving. Here are some practical but important needs the wife should take into consideration and work towards fulfilling:

1. Keep his shirts clean and in the proper place.
2. Keep a stack of handkerchiefs clean and ready.
3. Keep his socks clean, put together, and in the drawer.
4. Help hang his suits up if he once in awhile neglects to do so himself. Keep them cleaned and pressed.
5. Keep the house clean and orderly.

6. He should have a place that is his own, whether it be a corner or his own office. Keep it clean, uncluttered, and undisturbed by the other members of the family.
7. When he is on the phone, lower your voice and teach the children to be quiet at this time, as much as possible.
8. Prepare nutritious meals and keep mealtimes happy. Try to have dinner together as a family each day at the same time. This will take planning, but it can be done most of the time if you work at it. Use napkins and placemats, pretty dishes, and make mealtime cheerful. Have something positive to talk about.

Peter Marshall said, "Small deeds done are better than great deeds planned."[3] It is the little everyday thoughtfulness that counts. Caring and serving are essential for success. Paul wrote, "...by love **serve** one another" (Galatians 5:13). Love by serving, not waiting to be served, but looking for a place of service. In all that you do for your husband, do it as unto the Lord. "And whatsoever ye do, do it heartily, as to the Lord" (Colossians 3:23).

Your husband should be the first one to receive kind words from you. The virtuous woman was known by her spirit. Solomon described her by saying, "In her tongue is the law of kindness" (Proverbs 31:26). Frederick Faber expressed it well: "Kind words are the music of the world. They have a power which seems to be beyond natural causes, as though they were some angel's song which had lost its way and come to earth."[4] Kindness is love doing and serving. *Love in words, actions, and thoughts* should control your attitude toward your husband.

6. CONVERSATION

Your conversation is important. Your minister husband is influenced by your talk. It is important to talk of the Lord as the psalmist wrote, "My soul shall make her boast in the Lord..." (Psalm 34:2). Do not be down-in-the-mouth, but speak positively, on the upward swing. No matter what happens, look at a problem squarely and let your conversation include God and His promises. "...The tongue of the wise is health" (Proverbs 12:18). Yes, it gives new hope when there is despair, new life when all is crumbling, and calls forth old Bible promises in moments of discouragement.

Learn to be the unforgettable woman in your husband's life. Do him good, be aware, be alive, love, suffer gracefully, be happy and make him feel larger than life. Yes, learn to be the virtuous woman whose price is far above rubies, for Proverbs 18:22 says you are a "good" thing to your husband. Do the things that will make you a good helpmeet.

You are to minister to your husband's emotional and physical needs as much as possible. Try to say the right words to comfort and inspire him. You are his closest companion and he should be able to draw strength and love from you. Every woman has an influence; make sure yours is good, godly, and generous. Give to him honor, respect, and praise, and you will be following God's success formula. As you build him up and encourage him, do not worry about making him proud; there are enough bubble-poppers in his everyday work to take care of that. You just do what God says to do, and He will take care of the rest. There is not one scripture that instructs the wife to

31

criticize, tear down, and spread gloom. She is to be joyous and full of love, respect and good-will.

You fill a need in your husband that no one else can fill. You should be his chief inspirer, constant encourager, and up-lifter when he is discouraged. You hold an important position. Just because you are not in the limelight quite as much does not mean you are not important. You are important so do your job well. It is important to give him reassurances, hope, and confidence to start his day. Do your best to not let him leave home with a discouraged heart and drooping shoulders. Work at meeting his needs and pull together with him for the cause of Christ. Nourish him with warmth, love, laughter, and good food; be considerate and kind. Unselfishly work, not for a temporal reward, but for an eternal reward from the Father in heaven who sees all things. Rise above the petty things of the flesh and help your husband, as well as your children and all whom you touch, so that they may reach their greatest potential in God. Be an inspirer, a woman of faith and victory!

3

You and Your Children

"Children are an heritage of the Lord" (Psalm 127:3)

Children are a gift from God, and parents are to be good stewards over their children. God expects parents to love, train, and raise their children up in the way of the Lord. He entrusts them into their care and gives them many instructions on the right way to bring them up.

1. Teach by example. Someone once said, "The parent's life is the child's copy book." An ounce of example is worth pounds of advice. Parents must be careful of the spirit that they have toward their children because they are learning from their parents' example.

Teach them how to pray and to live a holy life. Start praying with them while they are infants, teaching them that God cares about them and loves them. Help them to understand the importance of salvation in their own personal life at a young age. Have Bible study and prayer together each day. Let your children see you pray and hear you talking to God. The old saying, "Monkey see, monkey do" is true. They will follow your example. Prayer and Bible reading together is *more* important than brushing their teeth and other things that parents emphasize. Put emphasis first upon spiritual things, and then on all the other important things.

Parents are instructed when to teach the way of the Lord: "And thou shalt teach them diligently unto thy children, and shalt talk of them when thou sittest in thine house, and when thou walkest by the way, and when thou liest down, and when thou risest up" (Deuteronomy 6:7). According to this, much of our living and our conversations are to center around God, His precepts and guidelines. The most important thing you can do for your children is to lead them to Christ. Help them learn to give themselves to the furtherance of the gospel of Christ, not only in action, but in their lifestyle.

2. Teach them to be responsible in work and in handling money. Let your children learn the value of a dollar and how to be thrifty and stretch their money. Do not give them everything they ask for, or they will not appreciate much of anything. Teach them to give to God in tithes before they spend their money on something else. They need to learn to be good stewards of their allowance, then apply the same diligence with the money they earn when they are employed on the job.

In teaching responsibility, teach them to be honest, loyal, and dependable and to show all the character traits that you desire in them by being that kind of a person yourself. Let your words line up with your actions. When you make a promise, be careful to keep that trust, or they will learn to break their word.

Children should learn early in life to be responsible for and to carry through on their assigned chores. If you do something for the child because he was negligent, you are teaching him that someone will always do it anyway if he does not do it. Whether it is feeding the animals, bringing in the wood, cleaning out the fireplace, sweeping the walkways, taking out the garbage, building the fire in the fireplace, mowing the lawns, cleaning their rooms, cleaning out the garage, picking up walnuts, or pulling weeds out of the flower beds, see to it that they do it. You are preparing them for adulthood and you want them to be responsible citizens who will carry through on what they are told to do. Teach your girls how to cook, set a pretty table, vacuum floors, clean mirrors, run the washer and dryer, polish furniture, make a bed properly, change sheets, clean out drawers, do the dishes—the list is endless. Teach your boys to stack the wood properly, build a fire in the fireplace, and let Dad teach them how to prune trees, maintain the car, and repair things. Some of the jobs mentioned above are interchangeable between girls and boys, but the main thing is to help them to do it according to their age as best they can and to carry through.

It is a good thing for parents to introduce their children to some form of musical training in their early years. It will give them greater music appreciation and enrich their life, whether or not they go on to become accomplished musicians.

3. Take time to listen. This is a lost art among many people. Oftentimes a person is talking and then thinking ahead to what

35

he is going to say next instead of really listening to what the other person is saying. People will say, "Yes, really?" or "Is that right?" without actually hearing what is being said. To really listen, you need to hear things that are not being said verbally. You will feel vibrations of suppressed anger or unusual excitement and know that there is something that needs to be brought out into the open and discussed. Giving of yourself requires your time:

T: Thoughtfulness and trust
I: Interest and intuition
M: Mindfulness
E: Eyes and ears—Your undivided attention

Listen to your children's grievances and then give wise counsel. If you do not, someone will listen to them and give them the wrong counsel. Listen to them tell of their school day, about the school's musical, and the part they have in it. Listen to them plan the big party that is coming up and what they are to bring. Listen to them share the misunderstanding that may have occurred that day, then help them to get it all right. Listen, Listen, Listen. Who do you want to counsel your children? Who do you want to give them advice? They have to talk, and you should be their first counselor and adviser.

4. Teach them to stand up for their beliefs. Teach them to be tenacious in their beliefs on Bible doctrines and to not let down, but to be unshakable in the Word of God. The other day our 16-year-old son, Nathaniel, was working in the walnut or-

36

chard with a professor from Delta College. He had previously bought the lot from us, and we were teaching him how to irrigate and harvest walnuts.

The professor later told my husband, "You can be proud of your son. He is firm in his religious beliefs in a commendable way." This is an example of how important it is to plant strong convictions into your children's hearts and minds when they are small.

Teach your children to love and to embrace the Word of God so they will stand fearless in the audiences of their world, whether it be friend, foe or king. Start training them when they are young to read and memorize the Word and make it an integral part of their life. Let them see *you* reading the Bible and devouring it. Do not let it be uncommon to see you with your head in the Bible, studying it and loving it.

5. Discipline your children. One must remember that children in the growing years are not yet oak trees. They are growing, stumbling, and making mistakes. Parents should help, encourage, and apply discipline to them when needed. You can understand them better than anyone else, so to you is entrusted the responsibility of leading them in the right way. The whole foundation for discipline is in the Word of God. It will never change or fail; it is a rock to stand upon.

Two important things to consider in discipline are:

A. *Be consistent.* If you laugh one day at a cute expression or a word that is undesirable and then punish the next day for the same thing, your child becomes confused.

B. *Be positive*. Give advice in a positive way, even when it involves the negative. For example, if your child tells a lie, do you say, "You are no good. You are naughty, and headed straight for hell"? Or do you say, "All of us were born in sin and that nature makes us do wrong things sometimes. Even though you were wrong to lie and lying is a terrible sin, you can ask God to forgive you and then seek to always tell the truth. You will make God happy, your parents happy, and yourself happy, because you will feel better when you do things right according to the Bible."

Some scriptures dealing with the subject of correction are:

1. "Correct thy son, and he shall give thee rest; yea, he shall give delight unto thy soul" (Proverbs 29:17).
2. "The rod and reproof give wisdom; but a child left to himself bringeth his mother to shame" (Proverbs 29:15).
3. "Chasten thy son while there is hope, and let not thy soul spare for his crying" (Proverbs 13:24).
4. "Withhold not correction from the child: for if thou beatest him with the rod, he shall not die. Thou shalt beat him with the rod, and shalt deliver his soul from hell" (Proverbs 25:13-14).

The Word teaches that "For whom the Lord loveth he chasteneth, and scourgeth every son whom he receiveth" (Hebrews 12:6). A child feels secure when he knows that he is loved enough to be corrected when he has done wrong. If he is not punished he carries guilt and becomes very irritable. Although there are different ways to discipline a child, there are times when nothing else will work but a good old-fashioned spanking. God put a padded place in the body's anatomy for that administration. Someone once said:

The older I grow the more I find
That the happiest children are those who mind.
Who know that somebody cares for their good
Enough to make them do as they should.

Every child is different. Some of them are naturally inclined toward spiritual things, others have a worldly streak. Some are meek and others are stubborn. You have to work with each one as an individual. Start when the children are young, teaching them to be obedient, no matter what, and to submit to authority. They may not always do it when they get older, but the influence and knowledge will be there and it will be hard for them to get away from their early teaching. Mother, teach your children to respect their father.

The psalmist gave a comparison between children and olive plants. He said, "Thy children shall be like olive plants round about thy table" (Psalm 128:3). It is interesting to note that fresh olives have a bitter substance which makes them unpleasant to eat. This substance is largely or entirely removed when they have been **prepared** for market. I like to think that children are fresh and unprepared for life and the parents are the ones who help them learn how to act, how to respond, and what to do in a situation. In general, they help make them ready to know how to face life when they leave the fold. Parents have some bitter tastes in their mouth during this process, but those

39

experiences can help them grow in the Lord and also help their children to mature.

The olive tree has many small flowers. Most of the flowers are imperfect, and fruit cannot grow from them. They give off much pollen, and the wind carries the pollen from flower to flower. Every variety of olive tree can fertilize its flowers with its own pollen.

This is why God compares children to olive plants. Just as the tree fertilizes itself, children receive nourishment from their parents. What a parent is and does helps to produce the fruit of the children. Characteristics, beliefs, mannerisms, and spirit unconsciously becomes a part of them. It may take a while for all of these things to emerge, but the influence is there and someday it will have its effect.

There is evidence that trees occasionally benefit if they receive pollen from other trees. As the olive tree receives pollen from other trees, children will also be influenced by outside sources. Some of the influence might be detrimental, but other influence will be for the good.

Harvesting of the olives **requires special handling**. You also will spend a portion of your life giving a part of yourself to your children. When it is time for the harvesting in their older years, they will leave you and start a new life and put into effect all the years of your teachings. This is a time of special handling. They are no more children, but young adults in their own right. You treat them differently than you did when they were smaller. They now have more freedoms, and you must trust them during this period. You will need to change your strategy and use different approaches in dealing with problems. They will resent being treated as children when they are old enough to vote. Treat them as you would want to be treated: kindly and with respect. Talk over their responsibilities and that which you expect of them. They should be adult enough to follow through with their responsibilities when they reach the late teen years. It is not an easy job the Lord has given us to do, but, "...**all things are possible to him that believeth**" (Mark 9:23).

During your children's older years, you will use discipline, instructions, and other methods to bend their will to God's teaching. The most effective method that will always combat worldliness, sin, and bad habits victoriously is godly living on the part of the parent. Sometimes there is a need for deep praying and travailing during the time that the children are in the house. They can turn a deaf ear to instructions, get angry at stern words, but they cannot stand travailing prayer. That is what reaches down into their very soul. Prayer goes directly by the telegraphy of the spirit, quietly passes unhindered through walls and locked doors, and affects their inner heart and will.

6. Learn to laugh with them. The scriptures admonish us to "Rejoice in the Lord always" (Philippians 4:4), and that "A merry heart doeth good like a medicine" (Proverbs 17:22). There are times when things are tense and nothing else but laughter will clear the air. The incidents recorded in the four Gospels indicate that the children all loved Jesus. Children do not like to be around a sourpuss. It is apparent that He had a kind and happy spirit.

Laughter is contagious. There can be a spirit of gloom and despondency in a room, and when a joyful person walks in and

41

begins to laugh heartily, pretty soon there are smiles on everyone's face. There are some instances when a parent can laugh and teach a lesson better than if he is stern and disapproving. I remember one instance as a child when my mother sat down with us, and we looked at a magazine that depicted the antics of a family with many children. Having six in our family at the time, we identified with the article, and rolled on the floor laughing. This has happened in my own family over certain situations, and it is like a breath of fresh air. Everyone relaxes and love seems to rest on each one in the circle.

DARE TO BE HAPPY

Dare to be happy—
    don't shy away,
Reach out and capture
    the joy of Today.

Life is for living!
    Give it a try;
Open your heart to that
    sun in the sky.

Dare to be loving, and
    trusting, and true;
Treasure the hours with
    those dear to you.

Dare to be kind—it's

more fun than you know;
Give joy to others, and
watch your own grow.

Dare to admit all your
blessings, and then
Every day count them
all over again.

Dare to be happy,
don't be afraid
**THIS IS THE DAY WHICH
THE LORD HATH MADE![1]**

7. Be home when your children arrive home from school. If this is not possible, have a trusted adult be there. Do not have them come home to an empty house; no one likes to come home to a cold, impersonal house. This is very important. Many kids get into trouble and feel like no one really cares when they constantly enter an empty house. Be there to iron out the difficulties and listen to the funny incidents that happened that day. Have a small snack prepared and something nice to drink. Greet them with a smile, a pat on the back, or a big hug. This will nip a lot of problems when they are small because you are there to dispel wrong thinking and a disgruntled spirit.

8. Help your children to feel privileged—as opposed to cursed—living in a minister's home. Your attitude goes a long way in the situation. Be careful of your conversation. Never talk derogatorily about the saints. In teaching your children about the privilege that is theirs, they should be taught not to abuse it, but to appreciate it and be a blessing. This is not always easy, for sometimes they hear, "Well, you are the preacher's kid and so you should not do that." They can get the idea that they should not do something because their Daddy is the preacher. It should be pointed out to them that they should not do a certain something because it is wrong to do it. Somehow they are expected to be perfect examples, and they are not always that. Some kids are better examples than their brother or sister, but again I mention that each child has a different temperament and personality. Some kids seem to be angels, always seeking to please; others are like rebels always championing a cause. This will reflect in their behavior and attitudes about life. Somehow you and your children have to live through the glass-cage years triumphantly through Christ. Teach them to do things because they are the right things to do. They are an example of the believer, not just because their Daddy is the preacher. Teach them the scripture: "Let no man despise thy youth; but be thou an example of the believers, in word, in conversation, in charity, in spirit, in faith, in purity" (I Timothy 4:12). Remind them of Eli's children who brought him shame because they did not live right. If they do not get behind their father's preaching, how can they expect others to do so?

Through all these "open" years you must have love flowing from your heart and a firm rod of discipline in your hand. Be consistent and faithful. I think there are more "ups" for your children than there are "downs." Point out all the blessings that constantly come their way: the fresh vegetables, nice baked pies, cookies, homemade bread and Christmas remembrances. There are many natural blessings given to them down through the years. Also, it should be made clear to them that their Daddy is looked up to and respected in a special way. It is an honor to be the child of a minister and they should be made to think so, and in turn give forth a special understanding and be extra kind to everyone.

9. Togetherness is important. The psalmist wrote, "How good and *pleasant* it is for brethren to dwell together in unity!" (Psalm 133:1). Note the exclamation point at the end of the scripture. When planning the family schedule there should be time allotted for the whole family to be together. Children need to be heard and listened to by their parents. They need to be able to tell about their day and get some things that are bothering them off their minds. If you choose an evening for this, it is good to use a few quiet scriptures and family prayer to end the full, busy day.

Plan to have dinner together each day as much as possible. Make mealtimes interesting. Keep calm and think ahead for some topics to introduce that will bring forth lively conversation. Read a good news magazine for the highlights of world events and bring these up for discussion. Interject something positive about the work of the church or the works and character of great people.

Do not allow arguing or negative conversation at the table. You have to work at this when there are several children growing up together, but it can be done. You are the key. Wise Solomon wrote, "Better is a dinner of herbs where love is, than a stalled ox and hatred therewith" (Proverbs 15:17). It does not matter if you have the best set table using pretty dishes with coordinated colors, and are dining sumptuously. If there is a spirit of animosity and ill will at the table it would be better for you to have only a salad and beans and live in a coarse wooden shack and have love and good will.

Another way to encourage love and warmth between family members is to make the most of holidays. Two important ones are:

A. *Christmas.* The manger scene is a must. This is what it is all about. The decorations, candied apples, caroling, gingerbread houses, programs, gifts, fires in the fireplace, parties for the underprivileged, open houses, candy making, cooking, and baking all are a part of this joyous season. We thoroughly enjoy the Christmas season, and our family thinks this is the best time of the year. Everybody is happy. Learning parts for the church programs, spreading cheer, laughing, and loving make it possible to let others know that *Christ is the reason for the season.* This is an exciting time of the year.

B. *Thanksgiving.* This is a quieter and more relaxed time and is one of our favorites. We read scriptures and have candlelight dinners, and have everyone share that for which they are most thankful. It is a time also shared with family members and friends. Through the years we have put up pictures of the pilgrims or of the early days of our country and have written out scriptures pertaining to Thanksgiving. It is important to do these things with your children.

All the other holidays that have a good meaning can be a time of family participation. You can teach love on Valentine's

Day by reading I Corinthians 13. The Fourth of July and Presidents' Day can teach patriotism and respect for our country and her forefathers. Do not only celebrate holidays, but take time off to go to the zoo, ocean, mountains, or other points of interest. Make life fun and exciting, and for the most part, kids will realize that being a Christian is a clean and exciting life. They will want to make it their lifestyle when they are grown.

10. Teach them proper ways of behavior. Teach them:
- A. To be kind to older people
- B. Proper telephone manners
- C. To be quiet in church
- D. Respect for authority
- E. Table manners
- F. Proper grooming and hygiene
- G. To do unto others as they would have others do unto them. "For all the law is fulfilled in one word, even this; Thou shalt love thy neighbor as thyself" (Galatians 5:14).
- H. To not grumble or complain
- I. Proper manners for all occasions

11. Let them know you love them. That's right. Kiss your children, touch them, and show love by the tone of your voice. I Corinthians teaches that love is not irritable. Human love can wear thin with an exasperating child, but that is why it is so important to be Christ-controlled and let His love flow through you. There is no limit in His storehouse of love. It is easy to give forth scoldings and orders, but be just as quick to give out praise and confidence for a job well done. Do not compare children with one another. Do not show favoritism. Let them know you love them even when they have done something wrong. Do not talk about a child in front of him as if he were just another piece of furniture in the room. Children have feelings too, and are even more easily damaged than adults.

Be sure they are loved, but not pampered to the point of spoiling. It is important for them to have attention, but not an overly amount. Someone once said, "Do not let your child feel like he is the center of the universe, for God is." There is a difference between loving a child and spoiling him. Children should feel they are an important part of the family, but not as if everything revolved around them.

You should pray every day for wisdom in raising your children to be God-fearing citizens that love Him and love His Word and doctrines. The Apostle James wrote, "If any of you lack wisdom, let him ask of God, that giveth to all men **liberally,** and upbraideth not; and it shall be given him" (James 1:5). Now stand on it. Claim it. That is your promise as a mother. He will help you when you do not know the answers. Confidence in yourself is shaky and will fail, but confidence in God and His Word is the basis for success as a mother. He shall help you!

HOW TO BUILD A HOME

The walls of a home are not built of wood, brick or stone, but of truth and loyalty. Unpleasant sounds, the frictions of living, the clash of personalities, are not deadened by Persian rugs or polished floors, but by conciliation, concession, and self-control...The home is not a structure where bodies meet, but a hearthstone upon which flames mingle, separate flames of souls, which, the more perfectly they unite, the more clearly they shine and the straighter they rise toward heaven.

Your home is your fortress in a warring world, where a woman's hand buckles on your armor in the morning and soothes your fatigue and wounds at night.

The beauty of a home is harmony.
The security of a home is loyalty.
The joy of a home is love.
The plenty of a home is in children.
The rule of a home is service.
The comfort of a home is in contented spirits...The maker of a house, of a real human house, is God himself, the same who made the stars and built the world.

Frank Crane[2]

4

You and Your Church

"He that is greatest among you shall be your servant"
(Matthew 23:11)

There are many opportunities for you to use your privileged position to work for God and serve others. In my 32 years of being a minister's wife I have done a lot of things: organized and led youth and adult choirs, played the organ and piano, sang for funerals, gone on visitation, worked in bus ministry, visited hospitals, taught ladies' classes, taught beginner, primary, junior, young people, and young married Sunday School classes, have been Junior and Junior High superintendent and Sunday School coordinator, have knocked out walls, painted, put up wallpaper and such. I've made peanut brittle half the night and helped sell it the next day. The list is endless; when you marry a minister you somehow are expected to know how to do it all, even when you do not.

Many times I have blindly gone into a new situation loaded with all kinds of helps, studying for hours to better equip myself

51

for the job, and God has always come through and helped me. The best rule or lesson you can learn is found in Colossians 3:17, "And whatsoever ye do in word or deed, do all in the name of the Lord Jesus, giving thanks to God and the Father by him." Do everything in the name of Jesus and do it with thanksgiving in your heart. You will be called upon to do many things, and some of these things will fit like a glove—they will be a natural for you. Other things will be a chore. You will not enjoy doing them, but if there is a need, do it as unto the Lord. "Whatsoever ye do, do it heartily, as to the Lord and not unto men; knowing that of the Lord ye shall receive the reward of the inheritance: for ye serve the Lord Christ" (Colossians 3:23,24).

You are privileged in the fact that you are married to a "man of the cloth" and you are his confidant, and in most cases able to be involved in the activities you like best. People look up to you and respect you because of the position. Do not abuse it. Every minister's wife has certain talents and natural abilities. These should be given to the Lord, and He will turn around and use them to bless the church. There are many ways you can be a blessing to your husband's ministry and yet find your own identity and feel needed.

As you grow older and more experienced, God may allow you to speak to your local congregation. If He does, humbly prepare yourself in prayer, fasting, and study of the Word as you listen to the voice of God for that particular time. It is a privilege to minister the Word to others and the opportunity should not be taken lightly.

One of my favorite activities used to be the part of service that we ladies do so well and that is in the kitchen. I looked for opportunities to have a big dinner in our home: dinners for college staff, cell leaders, board members, and others. These were important groups that needed to be together in a relaxed home atmosphere of love and fellowship. It was fun to cook for God's people and entertain them. The planning of the menu, setting up tables, decorating the house and lighting the candles, all became exciting because I was planning for the greatest people in the world: God's people.

When our church was smaller, we had dinners in our home for all the new converts every six months and we loved it. Your husband will thank you and be proud of you for helping to make things warmer and more personable among everyone. If you feel like you cannot do it alone, enlist the help of some willing sisters in the church.

We used to have our cell leaders, their wives and some of the assistants at our home for a time of fellowship and inspiration. I had a florist in the church decorate the tables and also get all the paper goods. A committee set up the tables and cleaned up all the debris afterwards. I did all the shopping and food preparation. Three ladies came early and did a lot of the last-minute preparation. A man in the church brought the barbecue sets and briquettes and barbecued the hamburgers outside on the patio. Everyone loved the fellowship.

You can be a part of your husband's ministry by helping put together a good dinner for some of his co-workers, assistants, or key leaders in the church. Plan as if you are planning for the best. It is important for leaders to have a good feeling among themselves. You can help promote this by your serving in this area of hospitality and by being warm and loving to everyone.

Now that I am involved more in writing, leading prayer groups, and speaking, I have many more people helping me. In fact, they do most everything when we plan for the larger groups. God has blessed me with willing workers, so we bless the kingdom of God together,

Some other important things to be considered are:

1. Where should the minister's wife sit during a church service? If you are not on the organ or piano bench, you should sit up towards the front. Get in where the battle is the hottest, near your preacher husband and give him all the emotional and spiritual support you can muster. Because you are sitting in front, the way you worship and respond will be noticeable. The best rule of thumb for you to keep in mind as to your example in worship is, "Thou shalt love the Lord thy God with all thine heart, and with all thy soul, and with all thy might" (Deuteronomy 6:5). This does not give any place for lackadaisical worship. If you obey this scripture you will be a perfect example of how to worship. God will be the object of your affections and love, and you will not be worrying about what someone else is thinking because you will be seeking to please **Him.**

2. Do not copy anybody else. Be yourself. You will be miserable trying to be like somebody else. Do not try to be yourself entirely either. Put yourself in God's hands completely and let Him make you what He thinks you should be. Be yourself in the fact that you do not put on a front or try to be something you are not.

3. Be a blessing by watching for those that seem a little discouraged. Try to help them by giving them a warm smile, an understanding heart, and a listening ear and sometimes praying with those who need special prayer. Always be positive, standing on the Word in your advice or conversation. This is a good example for the ladies to follow. Never air your discontent or heartaches. Your heart fixer should hear those problems, for He promised to work them out and not put more on you than you could bear.

4. It is good to be in an attitude of prayer before church starts. Prepare your heart and get in tune with the will of God for the service. The devil will fight you on this. One time at 6:00 o'clock when I was almost ready to walk out the door, I heard a strange noise in the back yard. I glanced out and there were our horses and a sheep out of the corral running wild. Immediately I got our two daughters and our niece who was staying with us, and told the girls to go out and round the horses up and get them back into the corral. They had been with them earlier, and evidently they had not secured the lock properly. The girls ran out and worked and worked and were unable to get them in. Finally at 6:25, in a dilemma over what to do, I made up my mind. Our son drove me to the church with the baby. I told all the children to get those animals in, and as soon as they got them locked up safely, to come on to church and sit up front even if it was preaching time. I did not want the neighbors or the Humane Society after us, or the safety of the animals to be in jeopardy. I arrived at the church in a tizzy, although no one else knew. I calmly walked to the nursery and left Angela. Then I walked swiftly to the prayer room and flopped down on my shaky knees and tried to quiet my fast-beating heart. I prayed what was left of the prayer time and went to the organ and started playing, *"I don't know what you came to do, but I came to praise the Lord."*

It was not long before my husband looked over at me and said, "Where are the kids?" I mouthed the words, "Chasing horses," and he gave me a frown that said, "What is going on?" I just smiled and kept watching the front doors. About an hour later here came Sherrie in one door and Nathaniel in the other door. Right behind them come the other three girls, Stephanie, Elizabeth, and Sheila. They all looked a little wind-blown, but a look of accomplishment was on their faces. They got there in time for the preaching, and needless to say we heard a good lecture after church that night from preacher Daddy about closing the gate and locking it securely. The moral of the story: be in the prayer room on time as much as possible and at your post of duty regardless of what comes your way. (Do I hear a chuckle?)

5. Do the things your hands find to do with all your mind, body, and spirit. "Whatsoever thy hand findeth to do, do it with thy might" (Ecclesiastes 9:10). Whatever the need is, do it or see that it is done. Be a helpmeet, but never usurp your husband's authority or go over his head. There are many ways to enhance your husband's ministry in the church. I have mentioned some, but every wife has to find her place. As your church grows, your responsibility in one area can be given over to someone else so he or she can be a blessing and feel needed. You should not feel that you have to do everything. The greatest thing you can do is support your husband, get behind him in prayer and encouragement, and do anything he needs you to do to lighten his load. He will from time to time ask you to do certain things. Always try to do them to the best of your ability. Show your love and loyalty to him by being there when he needs you. Be sensitive to his needs.

Church activities such as visiting the sick and helping others should first begin with prayer on your part. "And the house was filled with the odor of the ointment" (John 12:3), when Mary gave her love and devotion to Jesus and broke the alabaster box. When the precious ointment of devotion to Christ begins to be poured out, those closest to you will be the first to know. There will be a different attitude and atmosphere. Singing will replace sighing, patience will replace quarreling, and grumbling and complaining will be a thing of the past. A feeling of love, peace, and gentleness flows out of a transformed personality, and as oil on troubled waters, it helps smooth all it touches.

The pastor is the head of the church, and man is the head of the home. But his position or authority does not render you useless. Women are loved and used by God in a great way. The very first evangelist or witness was a woman. She said, "Come, see a man, which told me all things that ever I did: is not this the Christ?" (John 4:29). The Head of the Church Himself sent a woman first with the tidings of His resurrection (John 20:17). Women cannot excuse their responsibility to the gospel just because they are women. You are not usurping authority when you are asked by the head of the church to teach or speak to a class or congregation. *Usurping* means "to take by force." Some ladies like to hide behind this excuse and not teach or help others because it is hard work and because discipline is needed on the part of the one that is doing the teaching. There is prayer, research, study, and discipline involved. If the Word has blessed you, and you are growing and maturing in the Lord, and the time is right in God's eyes and you are given opportunity to share the Word with those seeking more of the knowledge of God, how can you say no? You could make a difference in the destiny of hungry hearts reaching out to you if you would die out to self and say a total yes to God.

"He who learns and makes no use of his learning is a beast of burden with a load of books. Does the ass comprehend whether he carries on his back a library or a bundle of faggots?"[1]

You cannot teach successfully unless you experience teaching. One Sunday when I was twelve, we were on our way to Sunday School when my mother handed me a box of assorted objects and said, "Joy, you are going to give an object lesson in my department this morning. Get it out of that box." The wisdom of a mother saw my vivid imagination and potential and started me on my way. The method may have been unorthodox and if I would have known beforehand, I probably would have pleaded sick and stayed home. All of my angry protests fell upon a deaf ear. After I was in the primary department for twenty minutes, Mother announced that I would tell a story. I can remember the exhilaration of sharing a lesson with an interested audience. I was not only helping my audience learn and grow, but I was helping myself grow. We all grew together.

Not only will you benefit others, but you will benefit personally because the Word has a way of showing one what he is really like. It causes one to dig in and discipline himself to become the person God intended him to be. This does not happen overnight. It is a gradual process of walking close to Him and being sensitive to His voice. There is a breaking and molding that has to take place before one can impart the truth of God's Word to those who are hungry for more insight on the attributes of Christ and for practical Biblical application to everyday living. Jesus said, "I must work the works of him that sent me, while it is day; the night cometh when no man can work" (John 9:4). As He felt the urgency of the hour, so should we.

The important lesson for you to remember is that the man you married is the head, and he is responsible to God for the people he ministers to, and you are in subjection to him as your husband and your pastor. If he feels a need in a certain area and asks you to organize it, by all means agree to do it. You may go forth trembling, but God will equip you for the job. As you get into it, you will become so immersed in the needs of the people and the responsibility of the job that you will get your eyes off your own fear and rise above the jitters. The burden will then settle upon you in such a way that you will want to do the thing that you have been asked to do.

6. Do not neglect your family, husband, and home to do public *work for any long period of time.* There are times when this will happen. You will have to leave in a hurry and things will not run as smoothly as they should. But please, if this is an everyday occurrence, then you are too busy in the wrong things.

God wants you to run a well-ordered household, feed your family nourishing meals, share a listening ear, calm the fears of your children, and look your husband in the eye and listen to his plans and get excited about them. This all takes time. That is why it is important to organize and schedule your time. You are a steward over your time. One woman said she felt like a pie cut in six pieces that had to serve ten people. "Live life, then, with a due sense of responsibility, not as men who do not know the meaning and purpose of life, but as those who do. Make the best use of your time, despite all the difficulties of these days" (Ephesians 5:15,16, Phillips).

7. I Timothy 3:11 instructs the Bishop's wives to be grave, not slanderers, sober and faithful in all things.

Grave: "Deserving serious consideration: important; momentous."
Slander: "Defamation, oral or written, a false report, maliciously uttered and tending to injure the reputation of another."
Sober: "Calm and collected in spirit, temperance, well balanced. Not influenced by that which disturbs. Not inclined to levity or frivolity."
Faithful: "Full of faith in God. Firm in adherence to promises or contracts. Loyal."

In everyday language it means to have respect for your position and not treat it lightly. You should consider your position to be important and give consideration to all things that you do *before* you do them.

The way you act, look and think is important. You are influencing many people because of your position, and it should matter to you the impression or influence you have on others. You are dealing with tender souls, characters that need to be molded correctly, and impressionable minds. You are not your own, so do be careful how you handle the stewardship over the time, actions, and influence God gave you.

Your tongue must be under control, so as not to be malicious toward another. "Be holy in all manner of conversation" (I Peter 1:15). You should strive to be well balanced in all situations so as not to lose control in an important or trying manner, and regret later what you said. When you give your word, you must be faithful to that pledge. You want to be known as a woman that keeps her word and carries through. Seek to be faithful in all things: love for God, prayer, reading of the Word, love for your husband, keeping house, motherhood, friendship, and other important areas.

You may say it is a tall order. Remember I Corinthians 12:18 says, "But now hath God set the members every one of them in the body, as it hath pleased him." God chose and hand-picked you and placed you where you are. You have a special job. Every member of the body is important. "And if they were all one member where were the body? But now are they many members, yet but one body. And the eye cannot say unto the hand, I have no need of thee; nor again the head to the feet, I

61

have no need of you" (I Corinthians 12:19-21). God put us all in different areas of service in the church so it would function orderly and march forward triumphantly. Your role is important, and you cannot cop out and say, "I am not very important. It does not matter what I do or say." You are necessary to the body and it does matter what you do or say. Every member of the body has influence on someone else. Because of the important influence of the minister's wife, God gave several scriptures concerning her behavior and actions.

God expects you to give serious thought to the things in life that count for eternity, not just to think about having a good time, for that is secondary. One should not be seeking after pleasure, or to gratify the flesh, but should be seeking to further the gospel and its teachings so others might find God, and walk a new life by following the beautiful truths of His Word.

8. Seek to please God! It is impossible to please everyone. Hugh Murr once wrote, "The man who trims himself to suit everybody will soon whittle himself away."[2] Just do your best without compromising your ideals. Everyone will have their opinion, but listen to God, your husband and godly prayer warriors. Make yourself to be as courteous as possible to all the different personalities you will encounter. Try to love and get along with everyone no matter what! If mud is thrown in some circles, do not join in, for mud thrown is ground lost. Be full of enthusiasm even when circumstances would dictate otherwise. God wants you to be on fire, for He has promised to spue out the lukewarm, so learn to do what pleases Him.

9. Try to be a good listener. If your husband feels the need for you to help in a certain area of counseling, or if someone needs some down-to-earth, common-sense advice, listen carefully before spouting off an answer. James 1:19 says, "Let every man be swift to hear, slow to speak..." One preacher's wife said she felt like a cemetery, so many secrets were buried within her. Never break a confidence or gossip about another's problem. Keep your tongue with all diligence, and let your words pass through these three gates before releasing them:

THREE GATES

If you are tempted to reveal
A tale to you someone has told
About another, make it pass,
Before you speak, three gates of gold.

These narrow gates: First, "Is it true?"
Then, "Is it needful?" In your mind
Give truthful answers. And the next
Is last and narrowest, "Is it kind?"

And if to reach your lips at last
It passes through these gateways three,
Then you may tell the tale, nor fear
What the result of speech may be.[3]

Much is required of you, but it will be worth it. Remember in all that you do to be a woman of prayer. There will be times of crisis or times when a special need arises in conjunction with the church that you will feel totally exhausted in body, but peaceful in your soul for praying the burden through. This is a great part of being a minister's wife: to stand by his side and pray "until." Always stand strong on the Word and Bible principles. Let this rule your actions, thoughts, and conversation. Be a blessing and not a curse or detriment. Martin Luther said:

> I have held many things in my hands, and I have lost them all; but what I have placed in God's hands, that I still possess.[4]

5

You and Your Responsibilities

"She worketh willingly with her hands" (Proverbs 31:13)

Let's face it. Even though you are married to a minister you are still responsible for your house to be cleaned, meals to be organized and prepared, tables to be set, dishes to be done, floors to be mopped and waxed, clothes to be washed, dried and put away, shopping for needs, groceries to be bought, bills to be mailed, children to be chauffeured here and there, and your children's teaching and training. Do I need to list all the responsibilities of living that keep you busy?

No one woman can devise a plan for another with much success, for one cannot say, "Follow Step 1, Step 2 and Step 3, and all your problems will be gone," or "Do such-and-such and everything will be great." But you should have a plan covering the main household chores and other things that are important to you in your life. For further study there are some interesting facts on order given in my book, *The Radiant Woman*. A plan of organization should be simple and flexible and will need to be changed from year to year to fit the family's needs. Everyone's situation is different. In some homes the children have grown up and gone, so there would be an entirely different schedule for these than the ones that still have children at home. Some women share mobile homes and are on the road traveling with their evangelistic husbands, while other ministers travel a great deal and are away from home from time to time.

The important thing is for each wife to look at her home and evaluate what she needs to do to make it a haven of rest from a stormy world. Things should be done in as orderly a fashion as possible.

It is possible to cut down on needless activity by simply organizing. Shopping can be done on one day instead of running to the store every day. Keeping the laundry done so that there are not ten loads to do at once can be helpful. Cleaning thoroughly once a week makes for easier housekeeping the following six days. Some chores have to be done every day such as making beds, doing dishes and cooking for others, even when you do not feel like it. Some women have a helper come in and clean their houses for them. You have to do what is right for you, but whatever you do, there should be order.

It is very important that you make a happy home for your minister husband and family. This cannot be emphasized enough. Your home is the base for all things and is controlled by your attitude.

There was once a young man who learned how to approach life the right way. Being an elevator operator he met up with many different personalities. One gloomy Monday morning the elevator was filled with grumpy office workers. As the car

66

started up, the elevator man began humming a tune and dancing a jig. "You seem to be happy today," said one passenger glumly. "Yes, Sir," was the reply, "I ain't never lived this day before."

If you can adopt this kind of attitude, your life will be much more blessed. Seek to be joyful and it will spread to those around you. Abraham Lincoln said, "You are about as happy as you make up your mind to be." It is important for your home to be a place where wounded spirits are healed, broken hearts are mended, and characters are shaped. Music and laughter should ring through the rooms and resound from wall to wall. Missionaries, friends, ministers, relatives, and needy people should be entertained in this kind of atmosphere. You are showing your children how to treat others by the attitude you have in your home. Jesus said, "Inasmuch as ye have done it unto one of the least of these my brethren, ye have done it unto me" (Matthew 25:40).

Your home life is an important part of your life. It is a place where problems are worked out, discipline is administered, love is taught, and prayers are prayed. Your greatest influence is in your home. If there were more clean, godly, and happy homes we would have less crime and violence in the streets, and there would be more abundant life in the churches.

Although your attitude is important and it does reflect in your home it still does not take away all your responsibilities. You are not called to be a **super** woman, but you are commanded to do all things in the name of Jesus. If you can keep this attitude in mind, it will make your workload much easier. Conscientious young minister's wives are likely to set goals of perfection so impossible to reach that they carry a needless burden of frustration. Along with a schedule, you must learn to have a good sense of humor, because things do not always go as you planned. Unexpected company, broken-down equipment, sick saints and children can change everything. Learn to roll with the punches. Do as much as you can do in one day and relax, because if you do not get it done today you can rest assured it will be waiting for you tomorrow. If you get frustrated and easily angered over your schedule or someone not helping to keep things spotless, you are defeating your purpose. Remember, in a few years you will have a deafeningly quiet house that is spotless and untouched; so smile and put up with a little clutter and disorder while those precious children are around your table. Spirits and hearts of loved ones are more important than a rigid schedule and an unbending attitude on your part.

A woman's life is regulated partly by a monthly cycle. She may find there are times when she is more depressed, tired, cranky, and more likely to succumb to illness than at other times. If she is aware of this, as much as possible, she can schedule fewer activities which demand physical and emotional energy for that week.

Your energy level is determined by several factors, which include your body makeup, personality, and metabolism pattern. During all of life a woman's energy level is greatly affected by her mental attitude. I'm sure you can recall sometimes how difficult it was to get the house clean, but when your husband called and said he had some people he was bringing over in a few minutes, you were suddenly *motivated*. You were able to do in minutes what took you hours to do before. Your feet fairly fly when you become motivated.

Emotions also play an important part in a person's total energy output. "Fatigue has many faces: the frustrated, the bored, the lonely, those who suffer from inability to love or make love, the genuinely overworked, those who love with secret fear or guilt, and those who try to be all things to all people."[1]

Life is full of problems, perplexities, and tensions which cannot always be solved by self alone. But the Christian has a resource always available. God cares. The prophet Isaiah was inspired to write these inspirational words:

> He giveth power to the faint; and to them that have no might he increaseth strength. But they that wait upon the Lord shall renew their strength; they shall mount up with wings as eagles; they shall run, and not be weary; and they shall walk, and not faint (Isaiah 40:29,31).

> For I the Lord thy God will hold thy right hand, saying unto thee, **Fear not: I will help thee** (Isaiah 41:13).

This is the secret. *I will help thee.* You are not alone. The Lord is always present to help you live a successful life, full of order and light.

Remember, every woman has a different temperament and personality. Some are go-getters who always have a new project going and are quick in their actions, able to get a lot accomplished in a short time. There are other women that are slower about doing things, content to do the needful things, but

69

who do not enjoy starting a lot of extra projects. Whatever category you fit into, do not put your home and family into the background, for they are what life is all about. It is your privilege and responsibility to help them be their best and reach their potential in God. God ministers to your family and others through your hands and heart. If you want to be happy, learn to do for others and how to encourage them. In so doing a chain reaction is set in motion, and you become a happier and better person. It is the law of God. Do not ignore God's formula for true living.

> One of the most tragic things I know about human nature is that all of us tend to put off living. We dream of some magical rose garden over the horizon—instead of enjoying the roses that are blooming outside our window today.[2]

Do it today. Do not dream of how organized or happy you will be tomorrow or when the children are older, but learn to make the best of every situation. You can always find flaws and imperfections in every situation you are in, but set your eyes on the good and positive and seek to make your "world" a better place to live.

Start with you and your inner man. Do you like the way you are? If not, you need to wash away the spidery webs of discontent that are in your brain and replace them with thoughts from the exciting Word of God. Joshua gives the success formula:

> Only be thou strong and very courageous that thou mayest **OBSERVE** to do according to all the law. Turn not from it

to the right hand or to the left, that thou mayest prosper whithersoever thou goest. This book of the law shall not depart out of thy **MOUTH**; but thou shalt **MEDITATE** therein day and night, that thou mayest **OBSERVE** to do according to all that is written therein; for then thou shalt make thy way prosperous and then thou shalt **HAVE GOOD SUCCESS**. (Joshua 1:7,8).

His Word is exciting, life-giving and inspirational. Fill your whole being with it and you can do all things through **Christ**.

Thank God every morning when you get up that you have something to do which must be done, whether you like it or not. Being forced to work, and forced to do your best, will breed in you temperance, self-control, diligence, strength of will, content, and a hundred other virtues which the idle never know.[3]

6

You and Your Alone Time

"Sit still, my daughter" (Ruth 3:18)

I once heard the story about two men from the western civilization who went to a certain part of Africa to search for valuable minerals and rocks beneath the earth. It was difficult to get to that area without a native guide. The guides had to break the trail and lead the way because there was no map to follow. After two days of hard pushing and hacking undergrowth, the men became exhausted and sat down to rest. After an hour or so, the impatient, hard-driving men from the western world jumped up and said, "Let's go," but the natives continued to sit there. The men talked through the interpreter to the guides and tried to urge them and compel them to get up and go. Nothing could change their minds. Finally one of the natives spoke volumes when he uttered, "We have to let our soul catch up with our body."

Every once in a while in your busy hurrying to and fro, you need to sit down and "let your spirit catch up with your body."

You will feel more like going again after you do this. You will also have greater inspiration and accomplish much more than if you push beyond your endurance. Sometimes you can push ahead at such a fast pace that the Lord literally causes you to lie down. David said, "He maketh me to lie down..." (Psalm 23:2). Wouldn't you rather do as Jesus, our great example, did? He got away to be alone from the push and busyness of life. If you will do this you will not have to be made to lie down.

The following scriptures substantiate this fact:

"And when it was day, he departed and went into a desert place" (Luke 4:42).

"And when the evening was come, he was there **alone**" (Matthew 14:23).

"When Jesus therefore perceived that they would come and take him by force, to make him a king, he departed again into a mountain himself **alone**" (John 6:15).

"And seeing the multitudes, he went up into a mountain: and when he was set, his disciples came unto him" (Matthew 5:1).

Jesus dealt with the pressing of the crowd, the demands of society, and the ever-reaching hearts by departing for a little while alone. He knew the healing power of quietness. The prophet Isaiah wrote, "In quietness and in confidence shall be your **strength**..." (Isaiah 30:15).

Minister's wives need this alone time. It should not be an all-consuming thing, but a break away from schedules and other pressing things every so often is important. You can either sit in a chair rocking gently reading a good book with no interruptions, or take off for the day doing nothing except what you want to do. Drive into the country, park your car and watch birds flit among the trees and chirp merrily among themselves. Go to a small, quiet little town and stroll the street looking at antiques and interesting bric-a-brac. There are many things you can do that are relaxing and not associated with pressures, deadlines, and schedules. Whatever you choose to do, do it.

Get away from the busyness of life, the chatter of multitudes, the pressing of the throngs, the press of the needy and *"Let your soul catch up with your body."* Go sit by a quiet stream and let the water carry your problems downstream with it. Go to the library and get back in a quiet corner and let quietness seep into your heart. A walk through an orchard, a stroll by the sea with the pounding of the waves in your ears and the wind at your back—these are part of God's handiwork and somehow His sounds are comforting and have the rhythm of creation in them. Some wives may not feel this need as much as others. There are varying situations and circumstances in many different degrees.

"Silence is the element in which great things fashion themselves."[1]

Every once in a while put the smaller children in day care or get a baby sitter, and while the older children are in school, take a few hours' vacation. The whole family will gain from the investment of a time-out for mother.

MOMENTS OF AWARENESS

So much of life we all pass by
With heedless ear, and careless eye.

THE PRIVILEGED WOMAN

Bent with our cares we plod along,
Blind to the beauty, deaf to the song.

But moments there are when we pause to rest.
And turn our eyes from the goal's far crest.
We become aware of the wayside flowers,
And sense God's hand in this world of ours.

We hear a refrain, see a rainbow's end,
Or we look into the heart of a friend,
We feel at one with mankind. We share
His griefs and glories, joy and care.

The sun flecks gold thru the sheltering trees,
And we shoulder our burdens with twice the ease.
Peace and content and a world that sings
The moment of true awareness brings.[2]

At a time when trouble was brewing and there was unrest,
the Word of the Lord came to Isaiah for the people and said,
"Take heed, **and be quiet**; fear not, neither be fainthearted..."
(Isaiah 7:4). When you step back from everything for a short
while, you get a new grip on things. You see life from a differ-
ent angle. You have heard the saying, "I cannot see the forest
for the trees." It is hard to see clearly when you are right in the
midst of the turmoil. Let the cares slide away and you will gain
strength from your quiet time of mentally communing with
God. He is all-knowing and all-powerful, and is there to help
and give you new determination to do things right.

76

When you get back from your alone time, the telephone does not ring quite so shrilly, the baby is a lot sweeter, the other children are more cooperative, the housecleaning does not loom quite as large before you, and the church responsibilities are not as great as you thought them to be. Nothing really changed, but you did. You slowed down and allowed the spidery strands of anxiety to be swept away by the hand of the Creator.

This time of being alone should not be confused with your special prayer time you have each day. Prayer builds you spiritually and mentally, and it is a release. You cannot live without it. It is the very breath of life. But you also need a time that demands nothing from you. You are free to do or to do nothing. I have read stories of how the early pioneer women used their alone time. One woman would steal away into the barn and hide behind the hay reading her Bible.

Much of life's tension is caused by the hurry syndrome that is part of this generation. There is pressure upon everyone to produce more than ever before. There are so many meetings scheduled throughout the year that it takes a person's breath away if they look at a bird's eye view of a yearly calendar. It is important to mentally check yourself so as to not become caught up in the whirling merry-go-round to such an extent that you do not enjoy anything because you are hurrying so fast to keep up with everything. It would be good to commit this poem to memory:

I WILL NOT HURRY

I will not hurry through this Day!

77

THE PRIVILEGED WOMAN

Lord, I will listen by the way,
To humming bees and singing birds,
To speaking trees and friendly words;
And for the moments in between
Seek glimpses of thy great unseen.

I will not hurry through this day;
I will take time to think and pray;
I will look up into the sky,
Where fleecy clouds and swallows fly;
And somewhere in the day, maybe
I will catch whispers, Lord, from Thee![3]

It is your attitude about your responsibilities that needs to be enlightened. When you feel the load getting heavy and the pressure building up, take time off from the job for a few moments. Let up, step back, get your breath, take it easy and then you will be ready to go again. You do not always have to fly to Bermuda or the Hawaiian Islands to enjoy a break or a mini-vacation. You can learn to enjoy your own home.

VACATION AT HOME

You don't have to go on a journey,
You really need not travel far,
You can have a delightful vacation
At home, or wherever you are.

Have you tried taking life a bit easy

78

Have you tried making everything fun,
Have you gone for a walk in the moonlight
Or rested awhile in the sun?

Have you ever sought peace in a garden
Looking up to the blue arc of sky
Watching the bright panorama
Of clouds drifting lazily by?

Have you taken time out just to wander,
To go fishing perhaps, or just dream
Where the willows are trailing their branches
In a pool, or a gurgling stream?

No, you don't have to go on a journey,
You really need not travel far
There are all sorts of vacation treasures
Right at home or wherever you are.[4]

7

You and Your Creative Time

"But there is a spirit in man; and the inspiration of the ALMIGHTY giveth them understanding" (Job 32:8)

Within the heart of every person is a creative spirit or inspiration that often lies dormant. Every minister's wife should make time for her creativeness to emerge from the cocoon of potential. Whether it be writing, music, painting, needlework, or other things, there should be an outlet for your special abilities and creativity. There will come a feeling of fulfillment when you pursue the things you enjoy doing and for which you have a special ability. In order for you to be happy and not discontented, you need to have a well-rounded life. You cannot play all the time, nor pray 24 hours a day on your knees, nor work all the time. You are a steward of your time the same way you are a steward of your money. You pretty much choose what you do with your life. You need to have time for spiritual things, time for your responsibilities, time for husband and family, time for relaxation, time for personal hygiene, time for others, and a time for pursuing your creativeness or God-given inspiration, so plan your life accordingly and you will be a better minister's wife.

When you are immersed in doing things that are conducive to good living and doing what you like to do, you will feel fulfilled knowing that you are needed; in turn you will not be a drag on your husband. Instead you will enhance his ministry. Looking forward to something that you enjoy doing helps take your mind off of self and problems.

You are not being selfish or self-centered, but you are actually being good to your husband and children by being more content. You may say, "I do not have time." You have time for that which you make your priority. When I feel the inspiration coming on to write, I indulge myself and give in to that feeling, for it will never come back quite the same way. My pencils, pens, and notebooks are kept ready at all times, and for the past few years the computer has become an integral part of my life. I have carried notebooks in and out of cars and restaurants and have written in odd spaces of time whenever the wheels of thoughts started turning. Sometimes I am up at three or four in the morning just giving in to that God-given inspiration, letting my pen flow while thoughts tumble out. I enjoy writing and when I give in to the inspiration all I can think of is what I am working on. Problems and frustrations hardly seem to bother me as much when my mind is busy on these important truths. You live in a world of your own making. Your thoughts determine your destiny. If you think of Christ, He will lead you to victory. If you think doubt and failure, that is what you will live with.

What is lying dormant inside of you? Everyone has talent of some kind or something special to offer the world that would make it a better place in which to live. Let God release you and unlock the potential that is there. Let it out! Do not keep it locked inside of you.

When the light of life falls upon the life of men, secret powers begin to unfold, sleeping perceptions begin to awake, and the whole being becomes alive unto God (Jowett).

The following essay written by James Allen, entitled *The Inner Life*, will help you realize you can do more than you think you can.

You say you are chained by circumstances; you cry out for better opportunities, for wider scope, for improved physical conditions, and perhaps you inwardly curse the fate that binds you hand and foot. It is for you that I write; it is to you that I speak. Listen, and let my words burn themselves into your heart, for that which I say to you is truth: You may bring about that improved condition in your outward life which you desire, if you will unswervingly resolve to improve your inner life. There is no room for a complainer in a universe of law, and worry is soul-suicide.

By your very attitude of mind you are strengthening the chains which bind you, and are drawing about you the darkness by which you are enveloped. Alter your outlook upon life, and your outward life will alter. Build yourself up in the faith and knowledge, and make yourself worthy of better surroundings and wider opportunities. Be sure, first of all, that you are making the best of what you have. Do not delude yourself into supposing that you can step into greater advantages whilst overlooking smaller ones, for if you could, the advantage would be impermanent and you would quickly fall back again in order to learn the lesson which you had neglected. As a child at school must master one standard before passing on to the next, so, before you can have that greater good which you so desire must you faithfully employ that which you already possess..."If you have faith, and doubt not, ye shall not only do this...but if ye shall say unto this mountain, be thou removed and be thou cast into the sea, it shall be done."[1]

Reach your potential. Graduate to the next level of living. Do not stay in third grade all of your life, but learn the lesson there and go forward to the next opportunity. What is asleep inside of you, what lies frustrated, chained by laziness or lack of organization? Let it out! Use all of your talents and inspirations to became a better person and influence others toward God. But remember, talents and inspirations are coupled with discipline, hard work, sacrifice, and steadfastness. Work at it, plod with it, make room for it and someday it will shine. God will use it for His glory. Do not wait to face in your older years the woman you could have been, but be her now, utilizing every ounce of inspiration and creativity that God has given you!

"The greatest achievement of the human spirit is it live up to one's opportunities and make the most of one's resources."[2]

Many talented people never reach their potential because they are not disciplined to a cause or do not utilize all their resources that God has given to them.

8

You and Your Grooming

"For man looketh on the outward appearance"
(I Samuel 16:7)

School had dismissed for the day. A couple of teenage sisters had slipped into their father's office at the governor's mansion. It was during the time when bobbed hair was becoming very fashionable for the young ladies. The southern governor did not want his girls to have bobbed hair. On this particular day, they were both pleading with him for permission. One of them came out with that often-used remark, "But Father, everybody's doing it."

The governor asked, "Whose daughters are you?" After hearing them acknowledge him, he said, "Sure. You are the daughters of the governor. You do not follow the styles. You set the styles."[1]

Just as the governor's daughters represented him, you are an ambassador of Christ and His holiness. Paul said, "Now then we are ambassadors for Christ..." (II Corinthians 5:20). What you wear, how you wear it, the cleanliness of your hair, the state of your wardrobe, the condition of your body, and the cleanness that you portray is very important and represents Christ and His value system. Since you are watched and are an example because of your position, it is a part of your responsibility to put your best efforts into looking neat, modest, and presentable to any group of people whom you might meet.

YOUR WARDROBE

You should not always be complaining, "I do not have anything to wear." This shows poor organization and hit-and-miss shopping. How many times have you bought a pretty blouse on sale and then let it hang in your closet, hardly wearing it at all? You say you have nothing to go with it and never get around to purchasing something to go with it.

How does one go about organizing her wardrobe and feeling good about what she wears? First, you need to go through your closet and divide the clothes into seasons. Put away in a certain area clothes that are not suitable for the present season. Then go through the clothes that are left and organize them: blouses, skirts, dresses, suits, and sweaters each in a particular area. Put your shoes either in containers, original shoe boxes, or shoe racks. Have a place for flowers, belts, and other accessories. Then see if you need something to complete an outfit. If so, write it down. If you cannot wear a certain suit because you do not have the right blouse, take the jacket with you when you go shopping and shop for something to complement the suit. Complete an outfit so you feel good about what you are wearing. Sometimes you can switch blouses and skirts and make several outfits with a few things. Be creative! Some people have clothes hanging in their closet that are good clothes, but they do not feel good in them. Maybe the color is wrong. You may need to give some of them away.

At the beginning of each season take two or three days to organize your wardrobe for the season so you will not have to worry about what you are going to wear. This cuts down on needless shopping and on frittering away precious time. Get as many outfits as you think you will need, but keep the family's budget in mind. Shop for the appropriate outfits for the different occasions you will be required to attend. If you combine the past year or two's wardrobe with several new things, you will add just the right dash to your closet and will feel confident about having *something* to wear. An outfit includes more than just a dress, and the following should be given consideration:

1. Undergarments, hosiery, and shoulder pads
2. Shoes and purses
3. Blouses and belts
4. Suits and dresses
5. Scarves, flowers, or hats if you wear them
6. Jackets and sweaters

You should not wear a black slip with a white dress, and you should not wear tennis shoes with a dress suit. Are the clothes lined properly? Are they kept clean and ready to wear at a minute's notice? Do not wait until time to get dressed and then discover you do not have the right combination of things to go together to make an outfit, but plan ahead. When your clothes become soiled, either clean them yourself properly or take them to a professional cleaner on your errand day. Keep your shoes in good shape by using polish and the local shoe repairman. Your clothes can actually hinder you from having the right kind of confidence you need for a job well done. Mend your clothes, do not just pin them. Pins are for emergencies or temporary usage. If your clothes do not fit correctly, or for whatever reason you do not feel good about what you are wearing, you cannot be at your best. If this is your case, I would suggest you get busy and organize your wardrobe. Look at your closet with a critical eye and spend some valuable time and work at getting it all coordinated.

Let holiness be your guide in your choice of clothes. Can you worship God in them and still be modest? Are your necks high enough and your sleeves and hemlines long enough so as not to cause the Lord to hang His head in shame over the flesh that is being displayed? Does the way you dress incite lust in other men or does it show forth godliness? Yes, there are two systems or two kingdoms. Which one do you represent, the world's or God's? Christ does not need the world's system represented; Hollywood already does that. He needs godly holy women to represent purity and His kingdom.

THE BODY

You have just covered the body, but what about the body itself? Paul talks about your "glory" in I Corinthians 11. It tells much about you. You should wash your hair as often as needed to keep it clean. Some women will need to wash their hair more often because of the climate and texture of their hair. You, yourself, are the deciding factor. Your diet is also reflected in the health of your hair. You need lots of protein for it to have body and not to be limp, for your hair is 97% protein. After feeding it and keeping it clean, then arrange it in a becoming manner, using rollers or whatever you need to style it.

You should make it a point to keep your skin clean and never go to bed at night without cleansing your face very well. The dentist should be your friend, helping you keep your teeth in good condition. Do I hear a groan? Even if you do not have any cavities, you should try to have your teeth cleaned by a hygienist twice a year. Brush and floss often and keep sugarless mints or breath freshener on hand for public occasions.

You should care about the food you put into your body. You have only one body, and you can abuse it or protect it. You alone control what you eat. God gave you your body, and you should glorify Him by keeping it in good condition. It grieves God to see the way some people stuff themselves until they are miserable and about to burst. Smoking is harmful to the lungs and destroys the body, and this certainly does not glorify God—it is indeed wrong! Temperance is also mentioned in the Bible. Overeating or stuffing the body beyond the need of healthy living is dangerous to the heart and other organs of the body. You should eat moderately good healthy foods and not let foods feed your emotions. Sometimes an individual will eat because of stress, boredom, or problems that arise. Sometimes a person eats just because food is there. Eating also can become a habit, such as eating just because it is 12:00 o'clock, even if one

91

is not particularly hungry. A woman will feel better about herself when she is not overweight and will have more fun wearing clothes that compliment her.

The Apostle Paul wrote, "What? know ye not that your body is the temple of the Holy Ghost which is in you, which ye have of God, and ye are not your own? For ye are bought with a price: Therefore **glorify God in your body and in your spirit**, which are God's" (I Corinthians 6:19).

It is important to keep your body clean on the outside. A daily bath or shower with the application afterwards of deodorant, perfumes, lotions, and powders is needful. We were taught in *Body Mechanics* in high school that the minute you step out of the bathtub, you start perspiring and should immediately put on deodorant. Keep yourself clean inside and outside the body. Make sure you smell good. Make people want to be around you. Cleanliness is drawing.

Do not sit around all day, but get some action in those feet. Walk, run, jump, climb, ride a bike—do something. It will put a sparkle in your eye and some color in your cheeks. It will give you new energy. With all of the emphasis that is put on the external woman, remember that fadeless beauty is the inheritance of every woman who belongs to Christ. This kind of beauty begins on the inside, and its radiance actually transforms the outward appearance. "The king's daughter is all glorious within..." (Psalm 45:13). The sparkle in your eye, a warm smile, a radiant, fresh, feminine manner, and a gentle, peaceful spirit means more than your external features, even though they are needful of attention. Let your outward appearance measure up with your testimony of Christ's purity and the need for clean living. Do not contradict what you say by the way you look. Glorify your Father which is in heaven.

When David instructed Solomon concerning the building of the temple, he said, "The house that is to be builded for the Lord must be exceeding magnifical" (I Chronicles 22:5). In the New Testament, vivid instructions are given for the proper care of our bodies which are temples for God to dwell in. "Ye also, as lively stones, are built up a spiritual house" (I Peter 2:5). "Know ye not that ye are the temple of God, and that the Spirit of God dwelleth in you? If any man defile the temple of God, him shall God destroy; for the temple of God is holy, which temple ye are" (I Corinthians 3:16,17).

9

You and Your Example

"For none of us liveth to himself, and no man dieth to himself"
(Romans 14:7)

Dr. Howard Hendricks tells of a professor who made an impact on his life. He passed his home many times, early in the morning and late at night, and often saw him poring over his books. One day, Hendricks asked him, "Doctor, I'd like to know, what is it that keeps you studying? You never cease to learn."

His answer was, "Son, I would rather have my students drink from a running stream than from a stagnant pool."[1]

As the professor desired for those under his influence to drink deep from fresh ideas, may those you are responsible for drink from a fresh spirit. Do not allow your example to die or become stagnant because of a lack of discipline on your part. It is important for you to grow so you can help others to grow. The influence you have because of your position is not to be taken lightly. No man is an island or a part unto himself. With every person you touch, you will leave a part of yourself. There are many ways in which you can be an example. These are just a few of the important areas.

Be an example in personality. Everyone has certain temperaments and traits that are inherited or an integral part of them. There is room for improvement in everyone. Every minister's wife should be an example in friendliness. "A man that hath friends must show himself friendly" (Proverbs 18:24). You should seek to have a happy, sunny disposition, not too frivolous, but with enough humor so as not to be called a long-face or a sour-puss. You can be an example by your warm smile, kindness, honesty, and many other traits. The spirit of Christ shining through you is the greatest example that you can have.

Be an example in dress. This is covered in the previous chapter, so we will not linger on this. Dress modestly, but in good taste. Be aware of how you look. Do not dress sloppily or show an attitude of not caring how you look. The Apostle Paul instructed the women on how to dress: "In like manner also, that women adorn themselves in **modest** apparel, with **shame-facedness** and sobriety; not with broided hair, or gold, or pearls, or costly array; but (which becometh women professing godliness) with good works" (I Timothy 2:9,10).

Be an example in worship. You will unconsciously be a good example in worship if you worship God with your whole heart. When it is your desire to please Him first, and He is made Lord of your life, you will be setting a good example. Fall in love with Jesus, and let Him breathe new life into your heart, soul, and mind. Let Him wipe away disillusionment, disappointment, and bitterness. Let the fresh breath of heaven blow across your soul. Then you can lift your hands to the heavens and love Him because He made you whole.

Be an example in prayer. When your husband announces a prayer meeting to be held at the church, you should be the first to back it up. Always give yourself to prayer and have a reverence for prayer, which is communication between you and God. In the prayer room or in the altar service, if there is a need for prayer, be there. When you are approached by an individual with a problem, always try to say to him, "Let's pray about it, and I believe God will work it out." Let prayer triumph. If prayer is important to you, it will be important to others and it will color your life with victory. Your children are watching also. This is a privilege to be able to influence people toward God and eternal things. You are laying up treasure for every soul you influence towards God.

Be an example in your attitude...

• *Toward church programs and leaders.* Be positive about them. Help make their plans work. Put your shoulder to the wheel and back the leaders. If you hear grumbling or questionings, always point out the positive and help make a weak point strong. Do not be a gossiper! It is better to say too little than too much.

• *Toward your husband.* Treat him with respect. Never go over his head. Love him. The people will know and feel if you hold resentment or a lack of love toward your husband. If you lack the understanding of the true meaning of love pray that the Lord would help instill the principles of I Corinthians 13 in your heart. Let it penetrate the callused walls of your spirit and mind and **do what it says to do.** Love is not puffed up, seeks not her

97

own, and suffers long (verses 4-5). You are an example to the church family of true Christian love.

• *Under pressure.* You are being watched particularly when there is pressure or storm clouds hanging low. Keep your cool by being fanned by God's cooling agent: the Holy Spirit. He can keep you from blowing your top and saying unkind words. Keep your words sweet, for you never know when you will have to eat them. Smile and pray through the storm. Hold your husband's hands up in prayer during the battle. Always remember that after every storm there is a calm.

• *In the day of small things.* Someone once said, "Begin the way you expect to keep up." Do not wait until you reap a great harvest. The key is to act the same way now as you would when things are increased to a greater measure. Jesus proved this with the parable of the talents. He said in so many words, "Because you have been faithful over the smaller things, now I will make you ruler over larger things." He watches how you do your business, whether small or great, and rewards accordingly.

If you can remember that all things start with little things, then it is easier to remember to have right beginnings. If one builds properly he will not always have to go back patching things up. James Allen shares insight on this in his essay, *Right Beginnings.*

Life is full of beginnings. They occur every day and every hour to every person. Most beginnings are small and appear trivial and insignificant, but in reality they are the most important things in life. See how in the material world everything proceeds from small beginnings. The mightiest

98

river is at first a rivulet over which the grasshopper could leap; the great flood commences with a few drops of rain; the sturdy oak, that has endured the storms of a thousand winters, was once an acorn.

Consider how in the spiritual world the greatest things proceed from the smallest beginnings. A light fancy may be the inception of a wonderful invention or an immortal work of art; a spoken sentence may turn the tide of history. There are right beginnings and wrong beginnings, followed by effects of like nature. You can, by careful thought, avoid wrong beginnings and make right beginnings, and so escape evil results and enjoy good results...Loving, gentle, kind, unselfish, and pure thoughts are right beginnings, leading to blissful results. This is so plain, so absolutely true; and yet how neglected, how evaded, and how little understood.

It is the wise minister and his wife who realize that the people for whom they are responsible, to a great extent, can go no higher in growth than their leadership. You as a minister's wife should seek to grow in knowledge of the Word and constantly improve yourself. You and your husband as a team cannot fulfill all your dreams and visions alone, but it is your duty to help inspire the people to reach their potential and *everyone together* will help further the kingdom of God.

10

You and Your Hospitality

"He that gives becomes rich" (Haney)

God commanded the bishop or minister in Titus 1:8 to be a "lover of **hospitality**." Everyone knows where that puts the wife. The responsibility rests as much on her shoulders as it does on her husband. She becomes overseer of both the kitchen and the organization for good hospitality. Romans 12:13 encourages all Christians to be given to hospitality. I Timothy 3:2 also gives instructions for the bishop to be given to hospitality. *Hospitable* means "receiving and entertaining guests generously and kindly." *Hospitality* means "to give hospitable treatment."

The proper attitude should be, "This home is not mine. It is a gift from the Master. I am His servant and I pledge to use it as He so desires." Jesus said, "And whosoever of you will be the chiefest, shall be servant of all" (Mark 10:44). All Christians, especially minister's wives, are servants of the people and of Christ. The Apostle Paul wrote, "...by **love serve** one another" (Galatians 5:13). Some of you may think, "When I get the house all finished and buy all the furniture and knick-knacks I need, then I will extend hospitality and have people come for a visit." Remember, people are more important than things. Do not put things before people's needs.

About a year after we were married, some fine friends of ours came to visit our church to minister in song and to preach the Word. We had them come over to our house afterwards for refreshments and I will never forget the fun and fellowship we had with them. We did not have a stick of furniture in the living room so we sat around on the carpet. No, it is not things that are utmost, but it is caring and loving people. It is putting their needs and comfort above material things. It is essential to minister to one another spiritually through the love of Christ and show hospitality in everything with no thought of reward. Pleasure comes in the joy of giving, doing, loving, and serving.

I Peter 4:9 exhorts the church to "Use hospitality one to another without grudging." *Grudging* means "to be loath to give, to give reluctantly, to grumble, and to have ill will about what a person is doing." Why did we have to be instructed to show hospitality without grudging? God knew there would be times when the flesh would shrink back from offering genuine love and care for those in need. Philippians 2:14 says to "Do all things without murmurings and disputings." So learn to do it with a smile, for God has His recording angels watching. He knows every time you make a bed for that dear minister friend or give someone something to drink in His name. Do it well for you are doing it as unto Him.

Hospitality begins with your own husband and children. Greet them with happy feelings and a cheery "Glad you are home," instead of hostility and depression. Make them feel welcome instead of waiting all day to dump your frustrations on their shoulders. You should have already given your problems to Christ. Children are often greeted with scoldings. This should not be. The home should be filled with gentle considerations and much love.

I read the story about the little girl exclaiming before a roomful of guests, "Mommy, why aren't you this nice to us when people aren't here?"

The mother then asked the question, "Did it count, all this gracious open-house business, if I acted like a hellion the hour before company arrived? Wasn't there a glaring inconsistency if I really treated my children differently when outsiders were around?"

Open your heart's door with love and good cheer and then open your literal home with love and good cheer, welcoming with open arms everyone who comes to your home. Seek to lift them up and to make their load a little lighter. Help give them new hope, causing them to walk with a spring in their footsteps.

Light the candles, get out the deliciously prepared food, shine the furniture, vacuum the floors, and work to make your house glow. These things are important, but they are not the most important. It is important to light the candle of love in one's heart at the altar of God, and then radiate the warmth of His Spirit to others, and help lift a discouraged one or a lonely child. Give of your food, your love, warmth and kindness, for in giving you live. The following poem portrays what this chapter is all about:

TWO PALESTINIAN SEAS

One is a sparkling sapphire jewel,
its waters are clean and clear and cool.
Along its shores the children play
And travelers seek it on their way,
And nature gives so lavishly
Her choicest gems to the Galilee.

But on to the south the Jordan flows
Into a sea where nothing grows,
No splash of fish, no singing bird,
No children's laughter is ever heard.
The air hangs heavy all around
And nature shuns this barren ground...

Both seas receive the Jordan's flow,
The water is just the same, we know
But one of the seas, like liquid sun,
Can warm the hearts of everyone,
While farther south another sea
Is dead and dark and miserly—
It takes each drop the Jordan's waves
Until like shackled, captured slaves
The fresh, clear Jordan turns to salt
And dies within the Dead Sea's vault...
But the Jordan flows on rapturously
As it enters and leaves the Galilee,
For every drop that the Jordan gives

Becomes a laughing wave that lives.
For the Galilee gives back each drop,
Its waters flow and never stop,
And in this laughing, living sea
That takes and give so generously
We find the way to Life and Living
Is not in keeping, but in Giving!

Yes, there are Two Palestinian Seas
And mankind is fashioned after these![1]

Jesus said, "For unto whomsoever much is given, of him shall be much required" (Luke 12:48). You are given a place of influence and honor, therefore you should use it to give mankind hope, blessing, and salvation. Give back to God your home, talents, and time so He can take your little "lunch" and bless many. Give in hospitality and love to uplift and encourage and to deepen friendships. Help to inspire co-workers with a greater vision for the work of God's kingdom. Give and much will come back to you.

You cannot pluck a rose, all fragrant with dew, and give to someone without part of its fragrance remaining with you. You cannot light a candle to show others the way without feeling the warmth of that bright little ray.

105

11

You and Bible Women

"Be an example of the believer" (I Timothy 4:12)

A Biblical example of a great wife was Jehosheba, the wife of the high priest, Jehoiada. She risked her life to preserve the royal seed of Judah. In the midst of murder, hate and ill will she showed forth a great spirit, caring more for religious freedom and heritage than for her own personal life. She stole little Joash from his nursery in the palace when his father, the king, died. What faith in God she portrayed by her actions. She saw the need, but did not wait for somebody else to do it. She went forth with victory because she cared about the future of God's people.

Another great woman was Elizabeth, the wife of Zacharias, the priest. Both were such pure and righteous people in their actions that Luke penned these words about them: "And they were both righteous before God, walking in all the commandments and ordinances of the Lord blameless" (Luke 1:6). What a powerful testimony about this great couple—blameless and righteous, keeping all of God's commandments. I wonder what the God of the heavens is writing about the husbands and wives who are in the position of the priesthood—or ministry—today?

It was said of Lydia, who was among the first converts in Europe, that she was a great help to the apostles in the time of need. She always had an "Open House" for the early Christians and apostles (Acts 16:14,15).

Another great woman was Phoebe. Paul authorized her to be a leader and asked the early saints to assist her because she had been a succourer of many. *Succourer* means "one who stands by in case of need." She was so full of the spirit of God that her whole life became a perfume of service to those in leadership and to the work of the church. She was not the wife of a minister, but she felt the burden of these godly men and did everything in her power to lighten their load. Phoebe's example of service should inspire the women of this modern day, but her life could also stand as a condemnation to some who have less of a burden and desire to further God's kingdom on this earth.

What about Priscilla and Aquila? Their two hearts beat as one. Harmoniously, they labored together in the service of the church. They walked as one, for they had mutually agreed to put Christ first. Paul first discovered this godly pair when he came to Corinth from Athens where they had been driven by the edict of Claudius against the Jews: "And found a certain Jew named Aquila, born in Pontus, with his wife Priscilla" (Acts 18:2). At certain times this couple gathered the followers of Christ for worship and meditation and had church at their house. They will be rewarded as helpers to the ministry on that

Great Day. They gave everything that was theirs to the cause of Christ. Can we give anything less?

There are many great women mentioned in the Bible. Esther risked her life for her people. Dorcas was known to be full of good works and almsdeeds. There is Eunice, whose son, Timothy, became a famous evangelist and was a testimony both to his mother and his grandmother, Lois. There is the beautiful story of Hannah whose prayer brought results. We see her on the day of her greatest sacrifice, taking Samuel back to the priest, worshipping her God. What an example! Huldah of the Old Testament was known as a great prophetess and was much sought after in times of need and counsel. When Hilkiah the priest found the book of the law in the temple, King Josiah sent immediately for Huldah. She prophesied national ruin because of disobedience to the commands of God that were contained in the scroll. Her message brought about a revival, resulting in the reforms carried out by Josiah.

Jochebed was the mother who purposed in her heart that she would not bow to the commands of the king, but did that which was right in the sight of the God. She lived her life as unto the great God Jehovah in such a way that her two sons, Moses and Aaron, and her daughter, Miriam, lit their torches at her purposeful flame and marked history.

Mary, who excelled in the necessary spiritual qualities for the sacred task of bearing the Christ-child, was holy, undefiled, and separate from sinners. This great woman of purity and humility was chosen to fulfill the Old Testament prophecy concerning the coming of the Messiah. What an honor was bestowed upon her.

These women and many others were responsible for a portion of their "world." They stood upon godly principles and were dedicated to a cause. Nothing daunted them. They walked with simple but firm faith in their delivering God, believing Him to do great exploits! What impression are you leaving in the footprints of history? Are you giving your best to God and life?

THE BEST WE CAN

Face your deficiencies and acknowledge them, but do not let them master you. Let them teach you patience, sweetness, insight. When we do the best we can, we never know what miracle is wrought in our own life or in the life of another.[1]

Are you standing upon purity, righteousness, and worthy causes for Christ? You may not be well-known, but you are known in your "world." Will you be measured with the Phoebes, the Marys, Elizabeths, and Jochebeds, or will you be measured with the Jezebels, the Dinahs and Peninnahs who were petty, undisciplined, and misguided in their pursuits? What are you doing with the influence you have? Are you ruled by God-like character or by the flesh? What influences you? Are you ready to give an account to God for how your days are spent? Are you happy and pleased with what you are doing with your life?

With these Biblical examples of sacrifice, character, and purpose, how can one live a purposeless life with no direction, uncaring about others and their destiny? Is it not time to make an abrupt change in whatever you are doing and to evaluate your plans and motives to see if they are in alignment with God's?

There is dynamite in the hearts of women. There is power! If women could join together in one purpose and rise from depression, heedlessness, and laziness, then the world would need to watch out, for an army that would be undefeatable with God would be able to march. They would be marching with purpose, godliness, purity of thoughts and actions, working for a cause that would influence others toward Christ and His principles.

Rise up, ye women that are at **ease**; hear my voice, ye **careless** daughters, give ear unto my speech...Strip you, make you bare, and gird sackcloth upon your loins...**until** the spirit be poured upon us from on high... (Isaiah 32:9,11,15).

Are you one of those who are drifting through life with no purpose, no goals, no prayer life and have never changed their "world"? Are you never accomplishing anything that would influence others for Christ? Are you living each day as it comes, careless, without plans, or are you working toward goals for now and the future? Every facet of your life should have direction, including your children, church, and home. Do not live an aimless life, but become your best for God and reach your potential. Strip yourself of pretensions and false motives and come humbly before His presence and cleanse yourself. Stay until the spirit be poured upon you from on high. His spirit is powerful and inspirational. It will put a fire within you, and help you see things through His eyes and feel a portion of His heartbeat.

Some simple but rewarding goals are listed below. This list is not complete, but are just a few to jog your mind about things toward which you can work. Make your own goals, but do not stay in one place all your life or you will stagnate and be filled with remorse.

1. Make it part of your life to have time for prayer every day.
2. Make time each day for the reading of the Bible.
3. Do you desire to play a musical instrument? Take lessons and practice until you can play in church capably.
4. Are you a singer? How about your songs? Are they the same five you have sung for three years? Organize and get some new ones.
5. How is your temper? Do you control it, or does it control you? Does it need working on?
6. Do you have a love for reading and growing in the knowledge of the Word? Are you nurtured and well-read in the Scriptures so that you are able to teach others?
7. How is the situation with your children? Do you help them to define goals for themselves, or are you existing from day to day?
8. Is the home organized and run orderly or is there a frantic search for something every time you need it?

This is a very small list, but maybe it will prod you and encourage you to see the need to grow. Do not feel you are ever too old to learn and to be a blessing. Many people have continued to learn and contribute even into their nineties. Once you stop having goals and things to look forward to, you will die and shrivel up inside.

Be a woman of faith and belief. Jesus said in Matthew 15:28, "O woman, **great** is thy faith..." Here the Lord honored and gave special attention to a humble woman of Canaan and healed her daughter. Her great hope became reality. What is God saying about you? Would the summation be defined as a careless woman or a woman of great faith? What is keeping this year from being the best year of your life?

THIS YEAR IS YOURS

God built and launched this year for you;
Upon the bridge you stand:
It's your ship, aye, your own ship
And you are in command.
Just what the twelve months' trip will do
Rests wholly, solely, friend with you!

Contrary winds may oft beset,
Mountainous seas may press
Fierce storms prevail and false light lure,
You even may know real stress.
Yet, does God's hand hold fast the helm.
There's naught can e'er your ship o'erwhelm.

THE PRIVILEGED WOMAN

For weal or woe, this year is yours;
For ship is on life's sea;
Your acts, as captain, must decide
Whichever it shall be;
So now, in starting on your trip,
Ask God to help you sail your ship.

Alfred Lord Tennyson[2]

12

You and Your Community

"She reacheth forth her hands to the needy" (Proverbs 31:20)

Some strangers to Lord Shaftesbury were to meet him at a railway station. Asked they, "How shall we know his Lordship?" The answer is challenging: "When you see a tall man getting off the train and *helping somebody*, that will be Lord Shaftesbury! Sure enough, a tall man alighted from a coach, carrying in one hand his suitcase, and in the other hand the three bundles of a little, old working lady!"[1]

Lord Shaftesbury was known by his kind deeds. How do people see you? You may not personally be known by all the members of your community, but what you are is soon found out. You write a check and the clerk wants to know your husband's or your place of employment. As soon as you say the name of the church, sometimes the response is, "Oh, your husband is a minister," or "I knew you were a Christian." You are a marked woman the same as every other Christian woman, but even more so because your husband is the minister. It is unspoken many times, but the distinction is there. More is required of you. Jesus said, "Unto whomsoever much is given, of him shall be much required" (Luke 12:48). You are living with God's mouthpiece, plus you benefit from having a host of godly friends: other ministers and their families. You hear much good preaching and singing, and you have been given a lot of good influence; therefore, more will be required of you.

Wherever you go, be friendly and compassionate to others. Show forth the fruit of the Spirit to the grocer, the baker, the lady at the cleaners, the florist, and the unknown housewife. Notice lonely eyes, for they mirror a hurting heart. Care for everyone with whom you come in contact. It is overwhelming when one thinks of the vast multitude who are hungry, but the responsibility of the church is to bring them comfort and the healing power of salvation. If one could feel the heartbeat of Christ, pursue His goals, and touch those he meets with the gospel and Christ's love, then he could say his life was beneficial. An African proverb says, "Not to help someone in distress is to kill him in your own heart."

You may wonder aloud, "How can I reach our community better?" One way our ladies did this was by organizing classes for ladies. We started Radiant Life Classes in 1975 and have continued to have them almost every year since. The material we used at that time is contained in the book, *The Radiant Woman*. This has been a successful endeavor, but by no means has reached its full potential. We have great vision for what the future can do. This is a great way to teach ladies Bible truths pertaining to both things that interest them and their responsibilities. It also creates a friendly atmosphere in which to bring new ones and help them get acquainted with other church members. It is an open arm to the community and is a blessing to the church body by helping to establish new ones and winning others to Christ's gospel. These have been a real strength and a growing time for our ladies.

Since the church has grown we have changed our format. We now have Radiant Life Seminars during the fall or spring on two or three successive Monday evenings. These are always well attended and many great things are accomplished.

We open with one large session consisting of singing, worship, and a devotional speaker. Then we break for classes and later all come back in for a big rally and a special message, ending with a time of prayer and ministering. We provide babysitting and refreshments. Most of the classes are related to spiritual needs, marriage and family relationships, and growth based on the Word of God. Because these seminars are open to the community we have quite a few visitors, and have won several families through this outreach.

Two other things we have done, which you might want to modify to use in your ladies group, are *Esther's Court* and *Phillip's Daughters*. Esther's Court was an organized effort of fasting by the ladies. Leaders were appointed to reign over different months and their job was to enlist other women to fast one day a month or more. The result was that a lady was fasting every day of the year. We consolidated our efforts and it was powerful. Phillip's Daughters is an organization for teaching Bible studies. The leader of this endeavor has meetings with the teachers once a week to share notes, motivate and give new names of prospects to be taught. Several of our ladies have

117

taught with such anointing that during the Bible study, the ladies being taught have received the Holy Ghost. This is a ministry that many can do and it will enrich the whole body of believers.

The Lord has blessed us with another outreach which is affecting our community greatly: the ladies' prayer group. We have become a hospital to several in the community and people have come there to receive a miracle. Even doctors have been known to send some of their patients to us. God has now opened another door for us to pray live over the radio for one hour per week. We read prayer requests over the air and then pray fervently for them and there is always a special presence of the Lord that fills the studio and goes into the homes of all those listening. Over and over people call in and say they are feeling such a strong presence of the Lord while the prayer is going forth. The phone lines are jammed the whole hour. We not only pray but give the Word to them also. God has honored us with His anointing and many people are being blessed by His power. Sometimes while prayer is going forth, people will feel the power and will drive to the studio to have us pray for them personally.

At one time we organized prayer meetings throughout the city at strategic locations for several months. These were held in juvenile halls, realtors' offices, and other public places which were announced in the newspaper along with information pertinent to this endeavor.

There is so much that your ladies can do. They can light the candle of revival in your church, homes, and community. A woman that fears the Lord and includes Him in all that she does is sure to have a far-reaching effect. This is no time to sit and wait for something to happen. It is time to make something happen by getting on your knees and devouring the Word of God—then inspiration will come!

The Lord exhorted Haggai in the building of the temple in the Old Testament, "...Be strong...and work; for I am with you, saith the Lord of hosts" (Haggai 2:4). Likewise, a woman should be strong, not in her own self, but strong in the Lord. The virtuous woman is described as being strong. "Strength and honor are her clothing; and she shall rejoice in time to come" (Proverbs 31:25).

13

You and the Golden Years

"It is magnificent to grow old, if one keeps young" (Fosdick)

Let me grow lovely, growing old—
So many fine things do:
Laces, and ivory, and gold
And silks need not be new;
And there is healing in old trees,
Old streets a glamour hold;
Why may not I, as well as these,
Grow lovely, growing old?[1]

God has placed you in a special position of honor. You have walked many long miles with Him, and He has given you choice bits of wisdom that come only from age and experience. You may not be as busy as you were during the middle years, therefore, you may not feel as needed. Erase that thought from your mind; you are very much needed! Your steady walk is a beacon of faith to the younger faltering step. Your quiet, unhurried smile is a balm to an overworked and frustrated mother. You are part of a generation that is our heritage, and you are needed. Your presence is important and inspires others that they can do great things for God as you have done.

You now have time to enjoy some of the things you have dreamed of doing while you were younger, but were too busy. Some of the greatest works ever accomplished were given to us by men and women in their golden years. Grandma Moses started painting at 78 years of age. She never had an art lesson. For many years she embroidered pictures on canvas. When her fingers became too stiff to use a needle, she began painting in oil. She was 101 years old when she died.

Winston Churchill first became prime minister in Britain when he was 66 years old. Then at the age of 77 he became prime minister the second time. He retired at the age of 81. Proverbs 16:31 states, "The hoary head is a crown of glory, if it be found in the way of righteousness."

Hoary means "to be white or gray with age." If you have followed Christ and have walked in His way, you will be crowned with glory in your older years. Anyone that is crowned by this kind of glory will be deeply respected and held dear in the thoughts of all. Growing old in the way of righteousness is beautiful. *"There is nothing more beautiful in this world than a healthy wise old man."*[2] I like to translate that as being healthy in the knowledge of the scriptures with a beautiful spirit to match.

There is time to write your memoirs now. Some of the golden-year folks have had experiences that would inspire and prod others on to victory. These remembrances and happenings need to be written in book form as a living testimony to God's keeping power and glory. W. Somerset Maugham said, "When I was young I was amazed at Plutarch's statement that the elder Cato began at the age of eighty to learn Greek, I am amazed no longer. Old age is ready to undertake tasks that youth shirked because they would take too long."[3]

You are important to life. Old ornate buildings that have been kept in good repair are simply magnificent and beautiful. There is a feeling of history and awe as a person walks through the well-polished corridors. These buildings have proven over and over again that they will stand through storms and pressures. They stand in majesty and as a reminder of the early days of a country's history. Likewise, the older men and women stand as a testimony to the younger that life is beautiful when it is given over to Jesus Christ. There is a serene smile that adorns the countenance, and a gentle spirit that reaches out to enfold those who are frustrated, worried, and rushed. It is soothing to be in the presence of a great older person that has kept up the repairs on the spirit, and allowed smiles and joy instead of scowls and frowns to line his face. There are still important things for you to do. Opportunities exist, but they may seem to be a little more obscure than when you were younger.

For age is opportunity no less
Than youth itself, though in another dress,
And as the evening twilight fades away
Thy sky is filled with stars, invisible by day.

Henry Wadsworth Longfellow[4]

123

THE PRIVILEGED WOMAN

Insist upon yourself to be beautiful in spirit. As you daily commune with God and His presence floods your soul, remind yourself that His presence should always be in control. Seek to be cooperative and cheerful. Be an asset to your Creator and a blessing to all you meet. If there have been situations in life that have given you opportunity to became bitter, weigh them out and decide whether you want to be tense, unhappy, envious, and full of gall. Is it not better to be big enough in your spirit to let past mistakes and heartaches be buried in the cemetery of forgetfulness? Let the fresh breath of love blow through the windows of your soul and wash you clean and pure. You will be happier and will feel at peace with God, yourself, and your fellow man. Life is not long enough to harbor resentments and evil thinking. Get into your spiritual dump truck and fill it with the things that have bothered you: hate, envy, resentments, pride, ill-will, broken trusts and other related feelings. Shift into drive, leave the town of suspicion, and drive into the sun-filled country and back into the dump-yard of God's forgiveness. Dump it all on Him. He will take it, forget about it, and then cleanse and make you new in Him. You will walk with a lighter step and feel years younger because you are not carrying the load of needless irritants that you had carried previously.

The following gives a good description of true youthfulness:

YOUTH

Youth is not a time of life....it is a state of mind. It is not a matter of ripe cheeks, red lips and supple knees...it is a temper of the will, a quality of the imagination, a vigor of emotions...It is a freshness of the deep springs of life. Youth means a temperamental predominance of courage over timidity, of the appetite for adventure over love of ease. This often exists in a man of fifty more than a boy of twenty. Nobody grows old merely living a number years; people grow old only by deserting their ideals. Years wrinkle the skin, but to give up enthusiasm wrinkles the soul. Worry, doubt, self-distrust, fear and despair...these are the long, long years that bow the head and turn the growing spirit back to dust. Whether seventy or sixteen, there is in every being's heart the love of wonder, the sweet amazement of the stars and star-like things and thoughts, the undaunted challenge of events, the unfailing child-like appetite for what's next, and the joy and game of life. You are as young as your faith, as old as your doubt; as young as your self-confidence, as old as your fear; as young as your hope, as old as your despair. In the central place of your heart there is a wireless station; so long as it receives messages of beauty, hope, cheer, courage, grandeur and power from the earth, from men and from the Infinite, so long are you young. When the wires are all down and all the central place of your heart is covered with the snows of pessimism and the ice of cynicism, then are you grown old indeed and my God have mercy on your soul.[5]

14

You and Your Depression

*"I am troubled; I am bowed down greatly; I go mourning all
the day long" (Psalm 38:6)*

There will be times when your eyes will seem like liquid.
There will be no stopping the floodgates of tears. Your chest
will be heavy and the load will loom enormously large and un-
fair. Some ways to gain victory during these times are given
below.

*1. Always try to see the lesson you can learn during a dark
time.* If you will lean on the Lord, stay close to Him, and con-
stantly commune with Him during the dark moments of your
life, there will emerge a valuable lesson beneficial to both you
and others. God's care during these times often seems more evi-
dent than when everything is going great, because there is a
brokenness and washing away of the outer crust. Tears that are
mixed with a "not-my-will" spirit reveal the finer things of
value. The Lord will draw nigh to those who have a broken

heart. Let these be your "growing" times. These are the moments, if the spirit is kept right, that you can become a little more polished and shiny as gold. When all is dark, when trials pile up, and when people seem unaware of your heartache, stay close to the Master. He will make something good come out of this trying time of your life.

Another benefit of being broken or feeling low is that it causes one to open his heart's eye, so that he will have more compassion for others in need. The spirit can be made more tender, merciful, gentle, and kind. One is able to identify with another's needs and heartaches better, and many times acquires a more understanding spirit and becomes less harsh and judgmental. So during these times let the spirit do its work in your heart. Learn the lesson and retrieve the jewel of wisdom from amongst the ashes of despair, the rubble of self-pity, and dark thoughts. Seek to find it. Fix your heart and mind upon the purposes of God and allow His wisdom to gradually fill all the corridors of your thoughts.

2. Accept unchangeable situations. There are some things that make your heart break, and you know the situation cannot and will not change. These are the times you learn to accept the concrete things and ask God for help and grace to live with an annoying or heartbreaking situation. If you will constantly ask God to help you overcome and to give you a right spirit, even though there are unremovable irritants in your life, He will help you. You will become as priceless as a pearl made by irritants that get inside the shell. Do not stiffen up and rail against God, but be Christ-like in your attitude and say, "Not my will, but thine be done."

3. *Learn during these times to be faithful!* While you might have someone join you in prayer, it is not always wise to broadcast your depressions. Become a better person by allowing the spirit of the Lord to minister to you. Be faithful in prayer. Be faithful in Bible reading. Be faithful in church attendance. Be faithful in your smiles, warmth, and joy. The tendency is for you to want to run or get away for awhile, but if you will stay faithful during the times of tears, hurt and depression, you will become strong in the Lord. If you can be faithful in the little things even when the winds of depression blow, He will make you ruler over many things.

You may ask, "How can I be faithful to my joy?" Joy is having a constant delight in the Lord. It is there to undergird you in the darkest night, for you have the consolation that God never changes and He is with you always. Several scriptures about joy connect it with a trial:

Beloved, think it not strange concerning the fiery trial which is to try you, as though some strange thing happened unto you: But rejoice, inasmuch as ye are partakers of Christ's sufferings; that, when his glory shall be revealed, ye may be glad also with exceeding joy (I Peter 4:12-13).

Count it all joy when ye fall into divers temptation (James 1:2).

Just do it in Jesus' name! Learn to thank the Lord in all things, for He is working something out for your good.

Be a good steward of your time and do not let temporary depression stop your faithfulness to the Lord's work, for faithfulness is that for which you will be rewarded. You must not do your responsibilities only when you feel like running, singing, or "hanging the moon," but you must also do them when you would rather cry than sing. Be strong in the Lord; smile and work steadfastly even when you would like to run away and hide. It is alright to hide for a short time, but not continually. You will find your solace in a closet hidden away from people, while on your knees talking to God. There is a release in prayer, a letting go of pent-up emotions that can only be compensated by God's sweet presence. Let Him heal the hurt and take away the bitterness.

4. Talk to yourself and win. You can talk yourself out of depression if you have done the other three things first. Weigh the pros and cons of the situation. Look at it with a pure heart towards God. Then talk about the good in the situation. Lift yourself up by your thoughts. Rebuke evil thoughts out of your domain by the power of the name of Jesus. Try to look at it from eternity's eye and not from the eye of the moment. All of these experiences are for your good if you are consciously walking after God. Paul wrote, "And we know that all things work together for good to them that love God, to them who are the called according to *his* purpose" (Romans 8:28). If God be for you, who can be against you? (Romans 8:31). All heaven is behind you if you have a pure or single heart towards God. You cannot lose with that kind of investment.

5. This will not last forever. "This, too, shall pass." It is temporary. Just as a paragraph has sentences, so does a life. Some sentences are long, some are short. Your life is made up of sentences, but they do end and the subject changes. It goes from depression, to wisdom, to happiness. A good story covers many emotions; so does a life well-lived. The Master Weaver weaves in the dark threads so the gold can be more vivid in His tapestry. It all goes together.

6. Learn to praise God through this time. When you are singing praises to Him, you cannot help but start smiling. Praise Him because He will not put more on you than you can bear. Praise Him when all is dark and there is no light in sight. It will not be long until you start to see a glimmer of sunshine at the end of the long tunnel of depression.

"...Praise is comely for the upright" (Psalm 33:1). It is a beautiful thing to give praise. Sometimes you will not feel like praising God because you are too bogged down in your own misery to utter heartfelt praises. That is the time to do as Hebrews 13:15 tells us to do. "...Let us offer the sacrifice of praise to God continually..." This is the thing that pleases God. He desires praise and gives extra blessing when it is given under sacrificial conditions. Turn depression into blessing by giving praise to the King of Kings and Lord of Lords.

So, remember:

131

THE PRIVILEGED WOMAN

1. Always try to see the lesson you can learn.
2. Accept unchangeable situations.
3. Learn to be faithful during these times.
4. Talk to yourself and win—fill your mind with the Word.
5. This will not last forever.
6. Learn to praise God through this time.

15

Good Food For Thought

"As he thinketh in his heart, so is he" (Proverbs 23:7)

"Just as there will always be people who are less successful than you are, so also are there those who've achieved more than you. If you are ceaselessly measuring yourself against others, you will always come out feeling like a loser."

"Try to accept what you are. There is dignity—and peace—in accepting what you can do without conceit, and in accepting what is beyond you without feeling shame. And no matter what your achievements, there is no dignity or peace without this acceptance."

"The moment is yours—cherish it. Life is only a succession of moments, sad moments and happy ones, dull moments and fascinating ones. All of these moments share one vital, wonderful characteristic—they belong to you. Savor the possibilities of every single moment of your life. Realize its value. These moments are the fine pieces that, taken all together, make up your life."

Hold fast to dreams
For if dreams die
Life is a broken-winged bird
That cannot fly

Hold fast to dreams
For when dreams go
Life is a barren field
Frozen with snow.[1]

A NEW START

I will start anew this morning
with a higher, fairer creed.
I will cease to stand complaining
of my ruthless neighbor's greed;

I will cease to sit repining
while my duty's call is clear;
I will waste no moment whining,
and my heart will know no fear.

I will look sometimes about me
for the things that merit praise;
I will search for hidden beauties

that elude the grumbler's gaze.

I will try to find contentment
in the paths that I must tread;
I will cease to have resentment
when another moves ahead.

I will not be swayed by envy
when my rival's strength is shown;
I will not deny his merit,
but I'll strive to prove my own;

I will try to see the beauty
spread before me, rain or shine;
I will cease to preach your duty,
and be more concerned with mine.[2]

"Blessed is the man who, seeing his own face as in a mirror and haunted with a divine discontent at the manner of man he is, goes on to perfection."

Henry Van Dyke said,

Are you willing to stoop down and consider the needs and desires of little children; to remember the weakness and loneliness of people who are growing old; to stop asking how much your friends love you, and ask yourself whether you love them enough; to bear in mind the things that those who live in the same house with you really want, without

135

waiting for them to tell you; to trim your lamp so that it will give more light and less smoke, and carry it in front so that your shadow will fall behind you; to make a grave for your ugly thoughts, and a garden for your kindly feelings, with the gate open?[3]

Phillip Brookes wrote,

Bad will be the day for every man when he becomes absolutely contented with the life that he is living, with the thoughts that he is thinking, with the deeds that he is doing, when there is not forever beating at the doors of his soul some great desire to do something larger, which he knows that he was meant and made to do because he is still, in spite of all, the child of God.[4]

FRIENDLY OBSTACLES

For every hill I've had to climb,
For every stone that bruised my feet
For all the blood and sweat and grime,
For blinding storms and burning heat,
My heart sings but a grateful song—
These were the things that made me strong!

For all the heartaches and the tears,
For all the anguish and the pain,
For gloomy days and fruitless years,

And for the hopes that lived in vain,
I do give thanks, for now I know
These were the things that helped me grow!

'Tis not the softer things of life
Which stimulate man's will to strive;
But bleak adversity and strife
Do most to keep man's will alive.
O'er rose-strewn paths the weaklings creep,
But brave hearts dare to climb the steep.[5]

"Isn't it true that a lot of us blame the road when it is really just a pebble in our shoe? We think that the whole road is rough. And, looking back over something that seemed extremely hard and rough, we wonder how we got through it so easily. The mental pebbles that we put in our shoes make the job hard—not the job itself. Once we get rid of the mental obstacle, our whole attitude is different."

Here are some interesting quotes from the booklet, *Snappy Sentences,* by Paul E. Holdcraft:

"In regard to the great Book, I have only to say that it is the best gift which God has given to Man" (Lincoln).
"It is impossible to mentally or socially enslave a Bible-reading people" (Horace Greeley).
"Getting **even** with a person means putting yourself on his level."
"The teeth may be false, but let the tongue be true."

"The best way to get rid of an enemy is to make a friend of him."

"Rip Van Winkle is the only man who ever became famous while he was asleep."

"The man who is set in his ways doesn't hatch new ideas."

"Don't be like a rocking chair—full of motion but with no progress."

"A lot of people have ability, but lack stability."

"The consciousness of duty done gives us music at midnight" (G. Herbert).

"To take the wind out of an angry man's sails, stay calm."

"When you brood over your troubles, you hatch despair."

"When you hear an evil report about anyone, halve and quarter it, then say nothing about the rest" (Spurgeon).

16

Nutshell Advice

"The wife see that she reverence her husband"
(Ephesians 5:33)

PART ONE: FOR THE WIFE

1. Your relationship with God is utmost. This colors all other relationships. If you have a close walk with Him personally, you will be successful in other areas because He is number one in all that you do. Therefore the Lord will give you wisdom to make right decisions and to direct your thoughts. He will help you choose right priorities because they will be founded on the Word. The Word and God are synonymous. Again let me emphasize daily prayer and daily saturation of the Word. Discipline yourself in these two areas, and you will grow in wisdom and knowledge.

2. Consciously seek to have the character traits of Christ in your life. Seek to be ruled by agape love and to please God.

This includes being kind, showing humility, keeping a peaceable spirit, treating people right, giving of yourself to hospitality, doing for others and spreading cheer, warmth and love. Be concerned and listen to others.

3. Seek God and wisdom. Do not seek things and material blessings; these will come to you as side benefits.

4. Whatsoever your hand finds to do, do it with all your soul, mind and spirit. Seek to do your best. Be filled with enthusiasm and erase half-heartedness whether you are seen or unseen. If you are faithful over the small things, He will make you ruler over larger things.

5. Be full of faith and have confidence in Christ. Never be pessimistic with anybody, especially your husband. Build faith and confidence; there are enough complainers sitting around waiting to stick pins in dreams and visions.

6. Do not be a quitter. Have purpose and a defined plan and carry through until it is finished. Note these three "P's" for success:
A. Purpose—a plan.
B. Persistence—a plot. Be determined. Never give up.
C. Pain. This includes sacrifice, tears, sweat, and toil.
These three points will cause you to be a conqueror.

7. Love, honor, obey, and be submissive to your husband. Be the unforgettable woman in his life. Make him secretly glad he is married to you.

8. Be a complement to your husband. Help him and encourage him. Do whatever needs to be done. Your talent will make room for itself.

9. Reach your potential. Do not die with dreams and music inside of you. Let it out and bless the world for Christ. Do not be a carbon copy, but find your own identify as long as it is in keeping with the Word of God.

10. Get your own life together before helping others successfully. Get order in your life in the following sequence:
   A. Inner
   B. Outer
   C. Home

11. In all that you do, keep a good positive attitude. You are what your spirit is. Give thanks in all things.

12. Learn to keep your mouth closed when it should be.

13. Be faithful in everything.

14. Do not be a possessive and jealous wife.

PART TWO: FOR BOTH HUSBAND AND WIFE

Almost everyone is interested in building good relationships. There is no magic wand that will make you a happy, radiant couple. It takes working together, here a little, there a little, building upon the right foundation. Ephesians states that the relationship between a husband and wife is as Christ to the church. Christ is the head of the church, and the church is under His direction. Christ does not push the church down or make it feel imprisoned, but He liberates it when His people walk in subjection to His precepts. Likewise, there are instructions for both the husband and wife to follow. Paul commanded both to love one another and also to honor one another (Ephesians 5:25,28,33). Only once did he refer to the actual word *love* on the part of the wife, in Titus 2:4: "Let the older woman teach the younger woman to love their husbands." I Peter 3:7 commands the husbands to honor their wife. Also, Ephesians 5:33 commands the woman to reverence her husband and that includes her love, honor, and respect. So it is important for both to love and respect one another, and to hold each other in esteem and to treat each other with courtesy.

Sometimes the wife will feel like she is not important because the man has the "important" job as the head of the family. This should not be. Every person has an important role to fill. God wants each of you to find that place and carry out your responsibility. Everyone involved will be much happier if they do it God's way. The wife is commanded to submit, obey, and reverence her husband! I Corinthians 12 explains how all the parts of the body are important and one cannot function very well without the other. Who is to say the car is most important or the gas that goes into it? The car cannot run on empty, and the gas is not useful sitting in a tank. It is only most important when it is being used. Consider the earth, the seed, and water. Which is most important in producing food? One cannot function without the other. There is a proper job for each to do. Likewise, there is a right way for the husband and wife to fill the role that God assigned them. If each does his Biblical part, all heaven will be behind them, cheering them on to a happy, well-balanced marriage.

Man was first in creation but last in transgression. Woman was second in creation but first in transgression. God knew women needed strong leadership, so He placed man as the head. The emphasis God placed on men was for them to love and honor their wives. The emphasis for women was to submit, reverence and obey their husbands.

Colossians 3:19 commands husbands not to be bitter against their wives. To be bitter means to be cruel, stinging, caustic, piercingly harsh, or distressing. Men have a powerful command of words, and God instructs them not to use their reasoning powers to cut down their wives, but to show them courtesy and honor.

Wives are not to be quarrelsome or contentious, but prudent and discreet. Remember, a nag is a hag, and a hag is hateful, argumentative, and gossipy. It does not take much horse sense to nag. The husbands should cleave to their wives and rule in love, not as dictators.

Following are twelve short building props to help make a great marriage:

143

THE PRIVILEGED WOMAN

1. *Work together.*
   "A mule cannot pull while kicking, neither can you." *

2. *Have humor and be joyful together.*
   "A good thing to have up your sleeve is a funny bone."
   "A merry heart doeth good like a medicine" (Proverbs 17:22).
   "Live joyfully with thy wife whom thou lovest all the days of thy life..." (Ecclesiastes 9:9).
   "Rejoice with the wife of thy youth" (Proverbs 5:18).

3. *Be truthful.*
   "A shady business never produces a sunny life."
   "Lies, like chickens, come home to roost."

4. *Trust one another.*
   Do not plant seeds of suggestion, dishonor and evil by suspicion and distrust. Plant seeds of love, honor, and trust. Lincoln said, "Suspicion and jealousy never did help any man in any situation."

5. *Be courteous and have a kind spirit.*
   "It isn't your position that makes you, but your disposition."
   "Life is not so short, but there is always time enough for courtesy."

---

* All quotations in this chapter, unless otherwise indicated, are from *Snappy Sentences* by Paul E. Holdcraft.

Sometimes the ones you love the most, you treat the most shabbily.

6. *Watch your temper and words.*
I learned a saying many years ago: "I keep my words soft and sweet, for I never know when I'll have to eat them."
"The emptier the pot the quicker it boils."
"What is in the well of your heart is bound to come up in the bucket of your speech."

7. *Take time for one another.*
Keep romance in your marriage. Keep growing in love.
"Little things are the hinges on which great results turn."
Never get too busy to show attention to one another. You have to take time for important things. It has been said a man never gets too busy to attend his own funeral.

8. *Be understanding.*
Be able to change a viewpoint if you are proven wrong.
"Some minds are like concrete, thoroughly mixed, permanently set."

9. *Stand together through storms and problems.*
Life will not always be rosy, but "all sunshine makes the desert."

10. *Live within the budget God has allowed you to have.*

"People who run into debt usually have to crawl out."

11. *Keep prayer in the home.*
"If there were more devotions in the home there would be less divorces."
Put God first, seek Him fervently, and He will help the perfume of love to linger in all the corridors of your heart.

12. *Enjoy the now together.*
"Some folks are so busy laying up for a rainy day that they cannot enjoy good weather."
Do things now together. Be kind now to each other. Do not say, "Someday things will be different, someday we will get along better, someday things will change."
Seek to change things now if there is a need for change so you can enjoy the years you have together now.

17

For Young Minister's Wives Only

"You can never have a greater or a less dominion than that over yourself" (Leonardo Da Vinci)

She sat across from me in the office very disturbed and upset. She was young, inexperienced, and up to her neck with "people," and she was just getting started. These were her words: "Being a minister's wife is not what I expected. It is too hard. Too much is demanded of me. The people do not respect me like they should. I want to give up. Help me, Sister Haney."

You may not have said these exact words, but there will be times when you will cry, "It's too hard. I wish I could get out of this." When you feel that way, come read this chapter again. The Holy Spirit is impressing me very strongly to write this. This will be my heart and His spirit talking to you, so it will be gentle, but straight.

Let us talk about some things that interest you. In talking to young minister's wives, I have found they seem to share basically the same needs. Every one is unique, but there is a familiar

147

pattern of thought or questions, although the situation is different. One of the questions that is often asked of me is, "How do you create a desire for spiritual things?" Many a young girl has said, "I want to be an asset to my husband, and be strong in the Lord as the virtuous woman is instructed to be in Proverbs 31, but I can't seem to pray that much or read the Bible. How do I get the want-to?"

First of all, let me ask you a question: What affects or moves you? Think back over your life and you will see that the things that touch you are usually things you see, read, feel or hear. You read a book and you cry. You see a little orphan girl with big blue eyes and you want to help her. Someone says something especially kind to you and you are moved deeply. You hear a song, a message, or a recitation and you cry or laugh. You were moved by what touched your senses. You are made up of emotions. In order to create a desire for something you have to hear, feel, see, or sense a need.

This being true, in order to create a desire for spiritual things, start reading books that inspire faith or that give you a desire to pray. You can go around the world in a book. Read, read, read, and read—then read some more! You are what you read, so read well. Examine not only your library material, but examine what you spend your time doing, and your choice of mental brain food. Exchange *Vogue* magazine for the book, *Ever Increasing Faith* by Smith Wigglesworth. Exchange *McCall's* magazine for the book, *Prayer, The Supreme Need of the Hour* by Andrew Urshan. You must read about whatever you want to influence you. It is your choice whether to walk the road of higher inspiration or Hollywood's wisdom which chains you to small thinking and gives you wrong direction.

If you do not like to read, then you have a major problem, but it can be overcome. You can train yourself to have a desire or interest to read, just as you train your small infant to do things he may not want to do. It will just become a part of his life. If you train him with rewards and ritual he will hardly know that he never did want to do it in the first place. But if you try to force him, constantly badgering him, it will be a long fight. The key for you is to develop a pattern of reading and then rewarding yourself for completing a good book. I have always loved to read, so this has never been a problem for me, but I have helped others who did not like to read and this method has worked for them.

Find a book that will help you and then establish a time to read it, even if it is a little each day. When you finish reading it, share the contents with a friend or with your husband. This will cement the good thoughts in your mind and you will be building for the future. It will be stored there forever. Then reward yourself with some small thing for accomplishing what you set out to do.

Remember to always be selective in what you read. Make sure it is scripturally sound and does not have overtones of New Age or other devilish doctrines. If you feel a check, ask your husband or an older, respected, godly friend. The most important thing for you to read is the Bible. Learn how to study it, for it is the most exciting book there is and it never grows old. Every time you read it, there is something new that pops out at you. If you feel the blahs concerning spiritual things, read a book or listen to a preaching tape on the subject that needs to stir you. Your thoughts become a tape recorder in your mind, and if they are not fed periodically, they can become stale and uninspirational.

When I first started eating honey, it was foreign to me. It had a strange taste. However, when I started reading the nutritional value of honey in comparison to sugar, it inspired me to continue on my journey of eating the better foods. After awhile, choosing honey was second nature to me. Sugar became the culprit or the outsider. Although I partake of sugar occasionally, honey is my first choice and it is so much more satisfying. I developed a taste for it over sugar. It is the same way with everything else. You can develop a hunger or desire simply by feeding it, educating yourself, and feeling the difference.

If after following these instructions for awhile you still do not like to read, be encouraged; books are now sold on tapes. You can listen to someone read to you while you are doing other things.

Secondly, the young girl said, "People don't respect me." I looked at her and said, "People are not required to respect you. You have to earn respect." This is true in any vocation. People will respect the office, but the person in the office senses whether or not he has the true respect of the people. The difference is clear and evident. How do you gain respect? What is respect? *Respect* is "to regard or treat with honor, to give esteem to someone."

I have been where you are. I was nineteen and a fun-loving teenager when I married my preacher husband. Overnight I became the co-pastor's wife of a small congregation. The people were kind and loving to me, and respected me because of who my husband and his family were, but I had to earn my own respect.

Then when I was 27, my husband was elected International Youth President. When I was 29, he was called to come back to be pastor of the church his dad had pastored for 34 years. When we came back, the former pastor's wife, my mother-in-law (a great lady), was still in the congregation. A church does not transfer its respect or loyalties to the new pastor's wife just because of an election. It takes time to establish rapport, confidence, and a track record on the part of the new pastor's wife.

So I say to you as I said to the young minister's wife: "Quit trying to get respect! Start thinking of others. Give your best to the work, the call, your family, to everyone you come in contact with and almost as if by magic there will be the respect you desire so much."

What you do every day determines the respect you have coming to you. If you want respect, you have to show respect; you receive what you give out. If you want love, kindness, and cooperation, then that is what you must show. Get your eyes on the first two commandments: loving God with all your heart, and doing good to your neighbor and others, and respect will come.

If you want to be miserable then always think of self, your position, what people owe you and what is coming to you. But if you want to feel happy and fulfilled, then you must do it God's way. Jesus said if you want to gain your life you must lose it first; then, and only then, will you gain.

The third important thing is this: You as a leader must affect people, not them affect you. If they gossip, you must not gossip back. Show them the better way. If they do not pray, you pray anyhow, for it is power. You must have something within you that drives you on. Do not depend on getting your inspiration from those around you. If you are blessed to have that— great!—but leaders must lead, not wait and see. You can be a Joseph and still come out on top, even if you have to wade through lies, jealousy, and spite. The leader of the pack always becomes a target, but you also are the first one to get there and taste the victory.

Fourth, you may ask, "How do my husband and I find time to be together—just the two of us—and have fun without the weight of the ministry upon us?" Just like everything else you do, you have to work at it. You need to put into your schedule time to be together without anyone else. You are young and probably do not have much money, but a restful stroll by the ocean does not take any money. Take advantage of the points of interest that are available in your area. Go out of town for at least 24 hours every quarter. Get the less expensive hotels. Forget everything and just laugh, sleep, love one another, eat and have fun. You will feel better and the people you minister to will feel your renewed strength. A harried mind and a strained relationship cannot be hidden long. Protect your privacy, for you are protecting the effectiveness of your ministry to the people. You are no different than Jesus. He at times withdrew, so must you in order to restore. A refreshed vessel is so much more refreshing to the people.

Fifth, develop goals. The best place to organize your thoughts and develop your goals is after a time of prayer, for then you will have heaven's influence upon your thoughts. You can and should want to excel. The Bible talks about being successful (Joshua 1:8). This, of course, is predicated upon the meditation and application of the Word of God. You can read something and not apply it, and you have only inspired thoughts. He who wins in the Olympics trains daily to win the coveted prize. It is not hit or miss, but it is a lifestyle. In the same way, a minister and his wife must develop a lifestyle of discipline and training. You must train your body, thoughts, habits, and mind to go forward and win.

According to Daniel 11:32, you can do great things if you know God. Knowing Him is the key; when you rub shoulders with greatness every day, it is going to rub off on you. If you want to play the piano, you must practice every day diligently. If you want to be effective in any field, you must train your mind in your selected choice. Above all things, *know Him,* and you cannot help but reach your goals.

You will hear negative voices that say some things are impossible, but choose to follow the Word. "Jesus said unto him, If thou canst believe, all things are possible to him that believeth" (Mark 9:23). The majority said that Fulton could not build a steamboat and while they were voicing their opinion, Fulton steamed by them down the Mississippi River. The crowd thought the Wright Brothers were crazy and said no one could fly like a bird. While the world laughed, two brothers gave themselves daily to their dream until they could fly. If you are not lazy, but are willing to discipline yourself and work daily an

153

inch here and an inch there, you will eventually reach your goals. The secret is to never give up!

There are times you will feel alone, even in a crowd, simply because you are on a different wavelength. You will converse with people, but there is no meeting of the soul. Most leaders or people that do anything worth remembering in life do not waste their time in trivial thought or talk. They are always chewing on a new idea or involved in a project that is bigger than they are. Great souls are people who are concerned with the intangibles more than the tangibles. The crowd is usually talking about clothes, other people, their problems, body, or things. This can be lonely to someone who is burning with desire to reach a world with the gospel, who has just had an experience in the spirit, or is bursting with excitement over an inspirational thought. Do not become discouraged. Just remember there are different levels of walking. There is the level of hell, the level of the gutter, the street level, the stair level, and then the sky level. The level you walk in will enable you to draw people to that level. The more you know Jesus, the higher the level will escalate, for to know Him is to fly. The more you humble yourself, the higher you will go with Him, increasing your effectiveness to change people and reach a world.

You also at times will feel less than your best, disgusted with yourself, and feeling like you will never get there. When you know you have not treated people right, and that your attitude is rotten, you can either be a Saul or a David. Saul tried to cover up and just went on worshipping, but David repented. In every situation always ask for forgiveness. "God, please forgive me," should be your daily prayer. Let arrogance or pride never be your bed-mate. When you go to church and the Word of God is ministered, and you feel the cleansing of the Word washing over you, showing you an area that you are weak in, respond to it. Be cleansed by the Word and by prayer and fasting and you will climb a little higher every time.

Another important point to remember is to guard your finances. Do not get into debt over your head by reaching for things that you cannot afford. Learn to live within your husband's budget and give God time to bless you with those things you desire. Financial problems put a strain on your relationship. Learn to be a good steward over what you have, then pray and trust God for everything else. It is exciting to watch how God answers prayers when you wait in relaxed faith. *Remember, you do not need everything you want, so discipline yourself and curtail your window shopping.*

No, it is not easy being a minister's wife, but it is a privilege only afforded to some. You have been chosen, so give it your best shot. You can do all things through Christ. What you become will be determined by your attitude. You can become a sourpuss or you can have a radiant glow. People do not put that expression on your face; you do!

The important thing is not who your father is, what your name is, or where you were born. The important thing is: what are you doing with what you have? Throw yourself into life with your whole heart and soul and begin to live abundantly! You can do it if you choose to do so.

Let me leave you with this story. If Leonardo Da Vinci were alive today, he would be called the product of a broken home. He was an illegitimate child and his father later married a six-

155

teen-year-old girl. For twelve years, he was brought up first by his grandmother, then by two aunts. With that start, it might be expected that Leonardo would have become a dull, sullen boy.

Instead, he had a curiosity about him that wanted to experience life. He was a "Wright Brother" in the field of aeronautics. He was a leading astronomer, geologist, engineer, botanist, and anatomist, as well as a famous author, illustrator, and psychologist. We know him for his famous artistic work, his greatest painting being *The Last Supper*. How could a boy with a bad beginning be so effective in his world?

How could John Bunyun, who was thrown into prison for a crime he did not commit, write such a masterpiece as *Pilgrim's Progress* and affect his world? How could a blind Fanny Crosby affect her world with her songwriting? It is this principle: Instead of the world affecting you, you affect it. You determine what you do with your life. Quit being down in the dumps, out of sorts, and full of self-pity. Start exploring! Read biographies of famous men and women. Do for others. Help heal the brokenhearted. Meditate on great thoughts and let those thoughts cause you to do something that will change your world.

This is not a book, only a chapter, so it must come to an end. Incorporate this chapter with the other chapters and live life to the fullest. There is so much to see and do. There are songs to be written, hearts to be healed, books to be birthed, children to be loved and trained, and messages to be delivered. New horizons are before you. Go forward and do it in Jesus' name! You are a winner; start thinking like one!

18

Putting It All Together

"Joy is not in things, it is delight in God" (Haney)

You are one person and are responsible over many areas: your relationship with God, yourself, your family, church and others. I have covered much material in this book. There is one last paragraph of insight I want to share with you. Where does your strength come from to do all these things?

"...The **JOY** of the **LORD** is your **STRENGTH**" (Nehemiah 8:10).

"Sing, O heavens: and be joyful. O earth: and break forth into singing. O mountains: for the Lord hath comforted his people, and will have mercy upon his afflicted" (Isaiah 49:13).

"Behold, God is my salvation; I will trust, and not be afraid: for the Lord Jehovah is my **STRENGTH** and my song; he also is become my salvation" (Isaiah 12:2).

"...My soul shall be joyful in my God; for he hath clothed me with the garments of salvation, he hath covered me with the robe of righteousness, as a bridegroom decketh himself with ornaments, and as a bride adorneth herself with her jewels" (Isaiah 61:10).

"The **LORD IS MY STRENGTH** and my shield; my heart trusted in him, and I am helped: therefore my heart greatly rejoiceth; and **WITH MY SONG WILL I PRAISE HIM**" (Psalm 28:7).

Sing while you work. Open the windows of your heart and let heaven's breath sweep away the seeds of discontent and grumbling. Sing unto the Lord a new song. "Yet I will rejoice in the Lord. I will joy in the God of my salvation" (Habakkuk 3:18).

"THIS IS THE DAY WHICH THE LORD HATH MADE: WE WILL REJOICE AND BE GLAD IN IT" (Psalm 118:24).

Let this scripture be your creed that you will live by. Let it be indelibly inscribed upon your heart. Live by it, walk by it, and it will not let you down. It is the way of victory.

Epilogue

As we come to the end of the book, let me add one more little thought that will help you when the bad times come.

I have been a minister's wife for over 35 years now and speak to you from a full life of experience. It is not always easy being a minister's wife. People tend to expect more out of you and your children than they do other people. Somehow your children are scrutinized and watched, and at the same time, many times they are not expected to receive any special favors. You are subjected to other people's feelings and prejudices just because of *who* you are, not by *what* you are.

There are areas in the spirit realm when you become a target for Satan's attacks because he will try to hurt the head of anything. That is what you and your husband are. There is the strong possibility that the time will come when you or your husband will be falsely accused and misunderstood. You will walk through lonely times when tears will be your constant companion. The heaviness of the work will be almost unbearable.

Being a minister's wife does not always seem like a privileged position. It has moments of heartache and disappointment. In it all, you will determine the outcome of everything by your attitude and by what you do during those difficult times.

The best thing you can do is to find a place of prayer and pray until! Lean hard against the Master. Try to rest in the Lord. With faith in your heart, trust in Him to bring you through shining like gold. Do not let life's trials tarnish you because of bitterness. Get out the Holy Bible and treat it with reverence and respect, and you will make it victoriously!

No matter how heavy the load, or how many difficulties go with the "job," it is still a privilege to stand in God's stead in behalf of so many souls. The key is to keep a pure heart and stay in tune with Jesus. He said if we were willing to drink of the cup that He drank of, then we would sit close to Him. Remember, it is not so bitter when He is your drinking partner.

You are on the front line of the battle and you will get some heavy firing from the enemy, but God and His angels are fighting right along beside you. If you will keep the upward look, you cannot help but go up. Remember, faith looks up, doubt looks down, and worry looks around. Keep looking up and someday you will be going up! What a celebration that day will be, but as the old song goes,

Until then my heart will go on singing.
Until then, with joy I'll carry on.
Until the day my eyes behold that city,
Until the day God calls me home.

Notes

Chapter 2

1. Helen Steiner Rice, *Just for You,* New York, NY: Gibson Card Compny
2. Ibid.
3. *Tapestries of Life,* edited by Phyllis Hob, Philadelphia & New York: A.J. Holman Company, 1974, p. 14
4. Ibid., p. 197

Chapter 3

1. Helen Lowrie Marshall, *Dare to Be Happy,* New York, NY: Doubleday & Company, 1972
2. *Lines to Live By,* edited by Clinton T. Howell, Nashville, TN: Thomas Nelson, 1972, p. 125

Chapter 4

1. Howell, p. 26
2. Ibid., p. 191

3. Hob, p. 174
4. Ibid., p. 68

Chapter 5

1. Dr. Marion Hillard, *Women & Fatigue,* New York, NY: Doubleday & Company, 1958
2. Hob, p. 24
3. Joe Mitchell Chapple, *Heart Throbs,* New York, NY: Grossett & Dunlap

Chapter 6

1. Hob, p. 31
2. Rice
3. Ralph S. Cushman, *I Have a Stewardship,* Nashville, TN: Abingdon Press, 1967
4. Howell, p. 130

Chapter 7

1. Hob, p. 53
2. Howell, p. 158

Chapter 8

1. Paul Lee Tan, ThD., *Encyclopedia of 7,700 Illustrations: Signs of the Times,* Rockville, Maryland: Assurance Publishers, 1979, p. 1268

Chapter 9

1. Tan, p. 1426

Chapter 10

1. Rice

Chapter 11

1. Howell, p. 162
2. Ibid., p. 95

Chapter 12

1. Tan, p. 568

Chapter 13

1. Howell, p. 9
2. Ibid., p. 11
3. Ibid., p. 10
4. Ibid., p. 10
5. Ibid., p. 12

Chapter 15

1. Howell, p. 36

THE PRIVILEGED WOMAN

2. Ibid., p. 44
3. Hob, p. 24
4. Howell, p. 158
5. Ibid., p. 180

The following books by Joy Haney can also be ordered from 9025 N. West Ln, Stockton, CA 95212:

Pressed Down But Looking Up	6.00
The Radiant Woman	5.00
The Elite	5.00
May I Wash Your Feet	5.95
Behold, the Nazarite Woman	5.95
When Ye Pray	6.50
When Ye Fast	5.00
When Ye Give	6.95
The Carpenter	5.95
Great Faith	6.00
How to Forgive When You Can't Forget	8.95
Philip's Family	6.00
The Privileged Woman	6.95
What Do You Do When You Don't Feel Like Doing What You're Doing?	7.50
Diamonds for Dusty Roads	8.95
The Dreamers	6.00
The Blessing of the Prison	7.50
How to have Radiant Health	8.95
Those Bloomin' Kids	5.95
The Seven Parchments	5.00
Women of the Spirit Bible Studies:	5.95 ea

Vol. I:	*Love, God's Way*
Vol. II:	*Faith, Prayer, & Spiritual Warfare*
Vol. III:	*All About Trials*
Vol. IV:	*Wisdom, Attitudes, Character*
Vol. V:	*Women of Compassion*
Vol. VI:	*The Power of Praise*